CW00926884

BRIGHTON'S BEST COOKBOOK

On the beach: a one-off gathering of Brighton's Best chefs on the seafront

Some of Brighton's acclaimed graffiti in North Laine, a city of vibrant culture as well as food

Contents

6	Introduction
10	64 Degrees
22	Bincho Yakitori
36	The Chilli Pickle
50	The Little Fish Market
62	The Set
78	Cin Cin
92	Plateau
104	The Salt Room
116	Silo
128	Semolina
140	The Gingerman
154	Terre à Terre
168	Curry Leaf Café
178	Isaac At
190	The Ginger Pig
204	Fatto a Mano
216	The Urchin
228	The Coal Shed
246	Riddle and Finns
262	Fourth and Church
276	Restaurant directory
277	Brighton's Best Restaurants
278	Index
280	Acknowledgements

Introduction

Brighton is the most vibrant city on the south coast of England. It hosts the country's second largest annual arts festival, the Palace Pier is the most-visited free tourist attraction outside of London, it's home to two universities, is the unofficial gay capital of the UK and boasts enviable shopping and nightlife. But until recently, it wasn't known as a dining destination.

There have always been great restaurants in Brighton: One Paston Place run by the late Mark Emmerson and his wife Nicole, stalwarts like John Burton-Race trained chef Ben McKellar's Gingerman group and Terre à Terre, and more recent openings including Riddle and Finns and The Coal Shed. Historically, though, the city appeared far more interested in drinking and clubbing than eating well.

But that all began to change about five years ago, as a new generation of young foodies emerged who, along with an influx of residents fleeing the impossibly high rents and house prices of London, created a market for modern restaurants that could bear comparison to the best in the country. The tipping point came in 2013 with the opening of 64 Degrees in Brighton's historic Lanes shopping quarter. Scottish-born chef and owner Michael Bremner had already made something of a name for himself at the well-reviewed seafront restaurant Due South (now Riddle and Finns on the Beach) but he emerged as a talent worthy of national attention at this tiny venue.

Emboldened by 64 Degrees' success, other chefs and restaurateurs followed suit, opening exciting and innovative restaurants including Dan Kenny at The Set and Douglas McMaster at Silo. It was as though Brighton's restaurant scene had hit fast-forward.

I founded Brighton's Best Restaurants in late 2015 with fellow Brighton-based food journalist Patrick McGuigan and Euan MacDonald of 60SecondReviews.com with the aim of bringing this new era to national attention. Although there were established food and drink awards for Brighton and Sussex, none focused solely on restaurants or produced a list of the best places to dine. As experienced journalists, we were confident that such as list would grab both the public and the media's attention and would raise the profile of Brighton's dining scene in a way that hadn't been achieved before.

We enlisted a 120-strong judging panel of chefs, restaurateurs, journalists, bloggers, broadcasters and business leaders, all of whom boasted intimate knowledge of the Brighton food scene. We asked them to vote for their seven favourite full-service restaurants and gastropubs that they'd eaten in within the last 12 months. We were keen that the list wouldn't simply be a run-down of the most expensive and gastronomically ambitious places in town, so we encouraged the panel to think about their experience as a whole and consider a local bistro or pizza joint for inclusion if they were the best of their type.

Announced in February 2016, the first Brighton's Best: Top 20 Restaurants list was warmly received by the industry locally and was the subject of national press coverage. For our second awards, we increased the size of the panel to around 150 members and added a panel of five 'Dedicated Diners' drawn from the general public. The 2017 top 20 are featured, in order, in this book.

In addition to the main list, we created a Best Sunday Roast award (won by Dizzy Gull at The Brighton Beer Dispensary pub), voted for by the public via Facebook. There was also a new award for the best dish served during the first Brighton's Best Restaurants' OctoberBEST festival (awarded to The Chilli Pickle for their Pork knuckle vindaloo, see recipe page 47). We were also able to add new categories of Highest New Entry (Cin Cin) and Rising Star (Bincho Yakitori) to our existing list of special awards that includes Best Chef (Michael Bremner, 64 Degrees), Best Barkeep (Matt Ottley, The Salt Room) and Best Welcome (David Toscano, Cin Cin).

Because the top 20 restaurants are so varied, the idea of a cookbook seemed the next logical step in the Brighton's Best journey. The recipes here cover everything including fine dining (Little Fish Market, The Gingerman, Isaac At), gastro-pub grub both Japanese (Bincho Yakitori) and British (The Ginger Pig), the best pizza (Fatto a Mano) and steak (The Coal Shed), inventive vegetarian cuisine (Terre à Terre), small plates (64 Degrees, The Set, Fourth and Church), hearty bistro dishes (Semolina, Plateau), stunning seafood (The Salt Room, Riddle and Finns, The Urchin), casual Italian dining (Cin Cin), cutting-edge natural food (Silo) and contemporary Indian cooking (The Chilli Pickle, Curry Leaf Café).

The book includes dozens of dishes that will dazzle your guests at your next dinner party and contains a whole new set of go-to midweek recipes to add to your repertoire (it would be invidious to pick out favourites). But because it also contains definitive recipes covering essential basics like stocks, sauces, bread, pizza dough and a guide on how to cook the perfect steak, it's pretty much the only recipe book you'll ever need.

Interviewing the chefs and restaurateurs for the introductions in the book was a fascinating process and has given me a new perspective on the Brighton scene. I learnt a lot about the characters that make the city such an exciting place to eat out in, and I hope you will enjoy getting to know them too. With the profiles, recipes and Peter Marshall's stunning photography, I believe Brighton's Best Cookbook is not just a really beautiful, useful and entertaining book, but one that captures a snapshot of an important moment in time in the city's culinary history - one that I'm extremely proud to have played a small part in.

Andy Lynes
Brighton

When Michael Bremner (pictured right) opened the 20-seater 64 Degrees in Brighton's Lanes in 2013, he kick-started a revolution in the city's restaurant scene. Counter seating at an open kitchen, a short, daily-changing list of imaginative small plates such as Salmon pastrami, and a modern, hip vibe. Brighton had never seen anything like it before. National restaurant critics raved, including Marina O'Loughlin of The Guardian who hailed 64 Degrees "the most exciting thing to hit Brighton for years. Actually, maybe ever."

"People label us 'modern British' and 'tapas', which I don't think we are. We just take British ingredients and do stuff with them," says Bremner, who 'reinvented himself' as a chef when he opened the restaurant. "It's a very creative place. We do a classic thing but use modern techniques, like making a hollandaise in a thermo blender and putting it into a siphon gun. We change at least one dish on the menu every day. The hispi cabbage dish always gets reinvented in one way or another, and there's always a braised meat and cured fish dish. Other than that, the menu is open to all ideas."

Born in the north-east of Scotland, Bremner began his career as kitchen porter in a country house hotel where his mother worked as a chef, then moved to London to work at The Orrery and Quo Vadis. He travelled to Canada and Australia before settling in Brighton to head up the kitchens at Due South (now Riddle and Finns), where he stumbled upon the name for 64 Degrees.

"We had a water bath, and after about six months I broke it. The dial got stuck at 64 degrees and it became a joke in the kitchen - 'what temperature do we cook this at?' - it just stuck with us," laughs Bremner, who also briefly considered the name 'Show' because of the restaurant's open kitchen.

In 2016, Bremner further cemented his reputation as one of the city's most high-profile chefs by appearing on the BBC TV professional cookery competition Great British Menu, where he scored 40 out of 40 for his Message to the Lodestar mackerel dish. In addition to being voted Best Chef two years running in Brighton's Best Restaurants awards, 64 Degrees has also topped Brighton's Best Restaurants' top 20 list in both 2016 and 2017, and is currently rated 16 in the National Restaurant Awards.

64 Degrees

Tuna, passionfruit, radish

(Serves 4)

This is an adaptation of a recipe that was introduced to the 64 Degrees repertoire by a Venezuelan chef called Egbaar. Leche de tigre - or tiger's milk - is a citrus-based marinade used to cure raw fish for ceviche. Here, we've replaced the more usual lime juice with fragrant passionfruit juice. This recipe works perfectly with oily fish like tuna, salmon or mackerel rather than delicate white fish.

1 litre cold filtered water
80g salt
400g sushi-grade tuna
1 tbsp olive oil
4 radishes, thinly sliced, to garnish

For the leche de tigre
200ml passionfruit juice
½ tsp diced Scotch Bonnet chilli
1 garlic clove, finely chopped
1 celery stick, finely diced
1 lemongrass stick, finely chopped
25g bunch coriander, roughly chopped
1 tsp mirin
dash of Tabasco
1 tsp sesame oil
¼ tsp xanthan gum (available from some supermarkets or online)

Bring 200ml of the filtered water to the boil, add the salt and stir until dissolved. Add the remaining 800ml cold water (the water needs to be cool enough so that the fish brines rather than cooks), then submerge the tuna in the brine for 40 mins. Remove the tuna and dry on kitchen paper. Coat with olive oil, then sear using a blowtorch until browned. If you don't have a blowtorch, quickly flash the tuna in a hot pan for about 20-30 secs on each side.

To make the leche de tigre, combine the passionfruit juice, chilli, garlic, celery and lemongrass in a mixing bowl and leave to macerate for 1 hr. Pass the liquid through a sieve using a ladle to squeeze all excess liquid out of the mix. Add the coriander, mirin, tabasco and sesame oil to the sieved liquid and chill for 40 mins in the fridge. Pass the liquid through a sieve again, add the xanthan gum and blitz with a hand blender. Sieve once more to remove any lumps. The consistency of the dressing should be somewhere between a liquid and a purée.

Carve the tuna to 5mm-thick slices, dress with the leche de tigre and garnish with sliced radish.

Hispi, hollandaise, truffle

(Serves 4)

This dish is real comfort food. Truffles are a bit of a luxury item and sourcing can be tricky; if unavailable or outside of your budget, replace with mushrooms or crispy bacon lardons. Serve this dish on its own as a light lunch, as part of a series of small dishes for dinner or with a roast instead of cauliflower cheese.

Make the hollandaise by melting the butter in a medium pan over a low heat, then remove from the heat and keep warm. Whisk the yolks and white wine vinegar in a bain-marie until thick and fluffy. Slowly add the melted butter, whisking all the time. The result should be a smooth, thick sauce. Season with sea salt and add a squeeze of lemon juice. Keep tasting the sauce until it is sharp enough.

Heat oven to 180°C. Dress the cabbage halves with the oil and pan-fry, cut-side down, for about 5 mins until dark brown but not burnt. Transfer to a baking tray and dress with the vinegar and a pinch of salt. Arrange cut-side up, place a knob of butter on each and roast for 10-15 mins until tender.

Serve half a cabbage per person. Pour over the hollandaise and finish with shavings of the truffle.

For the hollandaise
150g unsalted butter
2 large egg yolks
1 dessertspoon white wine vinegar
1 lemon

For the hispi
2 medium sized hispi (sweetheart) cabbages, halved
4 tsp sunflower oil
4 tsp white wine vinegar
100g salted butter

To finish
5g black truffle

Beef rib, carrot, crumb

(Serves 4)

You'll need to plan ahead several days, but this rich, hearty dish is worth the effort. You can buy the ribs as a set of four from your butcher. The meat can be taken off the bone after the long braise, or served on the bone if you wish. Here, the ribs are served with a salt-baked carrot and bone marrow crumb, but they also pair perfectly with buttery mashed potato, roasted onion or roasted squash. Bone marrow is now sold in some supermarkets, but if unavailable, just use the fat scraped from the cooked beef.

2 ribs from Jacob's ladder (short ribs)

For the brine
2 litres water
160g salt
4 star anise
1 cinnamon stick
1 tbsp coriander seeds
1 tbsp fennel seeds
1 tbsp black peppercorns

For the glaze
1 tbsp yeast extract
1 tsp pomegranate molasses

For the salt-baked carrots
400g flour
100g salt
250ml water
4 large carrots, cleaned

For the carrot purée
2 slices sourdough bread
fat from 2 bone marrows

For the bone marrow crumb
2 slices sourdough bread
fat from 2 bone marrows

To garnish
Pomegranate seeds
Micro coriander

To make the brine, combine the water and salt in a large pan, place over a high heat and stir until the salt is dissolved. Add the remaining brine ingredients, remove from the heat and leave to cool. Submerge the beef ribs in the brine and refrigerate for at least 8 hrs or ideally overnight.

Heat oven to 180°C. Remove the beef from the brine and pat dry with kitchen paper. Mix together the yeast extract and pomegranate molasses and brush over the beef. Place in a deep roasting tin and cover with baking parchment and then tin foil. Roast for 30 mins, then reduce the temperature to 100°C and cook for a further 8-10 hrs (or overnight). Leave to cool in the liquor, then strain the liquor into a saucepan and reduce on the hob to a thick, glazing consistency. Return the ribs to the glaze and heat through, making sure to baste all of the meat with the glaze.

Heat oven to 180°C. Make the salt crust for the carrots by mixing the flour, salt and water to form a wet dough. Wrap the whole carrots in the dough so they are completely enclosed, place on a baking tray and bake for 30 mins.

For the purée, put the sliced carrots in a pan and cover with the milk. Bring to the boil, cook on a medium heat until the carrots are soft then strain, reserving the milk. Blitz the carrots, adding the reserved milk a tablespoon at a time until you achieve a smooth consistency (you may not need all the milk). Season before passing through a fine mesh sieve.

For the crumb, blitz the sourdough into breadcrumbs in a food processor. Place in a hot pan with the bone marrow and fry until toasted, seasoning to taste.

To serve, divide the carrot purée between four plates. Break off the dough from the carrots, then place one carrot on each plate on top of the purée. Spoon the crumb over the carrots and place a piece of glazed rib alongside. Garnish with pomegranate seeds and micro coriander.

Venison loin, beetroot, walnut

(Serves 4)

4 medium beetroot, skin on
4 tbsp olive oil
500ml beef stock
1 tbsp pomegranate molasses
1-2 tsp Forvm Cabernet Sauvignon vinegar
800g venison loin, cut into 4 pieces
80g chopped walnuts, toasted
2 tbsp roughly chopped parsley

Heat oven to 180°C. Dress the beetroot with olive oil and season liberally with salt before wrapping individually in tin foil. Bake for 45 mins or until soft enough to easily pierce with a knife. Remove the skins while still hot - to do this without burning yourself, put the beetroot in a bowl of cold water and the skins should slip right off. Place in a dehydrator for 10-12 hrs or in a 100°C oven for 1-2 hrs until shrivelled.

Heat the beef stock and pomegranate molasses together in a pan over a medium heat, then add the vinegar to taste. Add the beetroot and reduce the liquid to a thick glaze so it coats the beetroot and forms a sauce for the dish.

Heat oven to 180°C. Season the venison with salt and pepper, then fry in an ovenproof pan on a medium-high heat for 2 mins or until browned nicely on the outside. Transfer to the oven and roast for 8 mins.

Rest the venison for 10 mins before serving with the glazed beetroot. Finish with the toasted walnuts and parsley.

You can usually get some variety of venison throughout the year, although most is in season from around October to February. This recipe is for fallow deer but red, roe, muntjac and sika deer are equally good - the latter three will be harder to come by. 64 Degrees sources venison from David Douglas at South Brockwells Farm in Uckfield, which is renowned for its game.

Rhubarb, lemon, shortbread

(Serves 4)

Rhubarb is a great English ingredient and is usually in season for over six months of the year. Choose crisp, firm, plump stalks with a good reddish colour. Fresh rhubarb will stay in reasonable condition for 1-2 weeks when refrigerated, and raw and cooked rhubarb freeze well. When preparing, be sure to wash and trim both ends of the stalks and discard the poisonous leaves. This shortbread recipe makes more than you'll need, but any excess raw dough can be stored in the freezer.

Make the custard by whisking the eggs, sugar and lemon juice together in a pan over a medium heat until thickened, taking care not to scramble the eggs. Add the gelatine and remove from the heat. Using a hand blender, incorporate the butter a few cubes at a time; the resulting mixture should be thick and glossy. Leave to cool, then stir in the cream. Divide the mixture between four serving bowls and refrigerate for 2 hrs or until set.

Heat oven to 160°C. To make the shortbread, cream the butter and sugar together in a stand mixer using the beater attachment (or by hand with a wooden spoon in a bowl) until smooth, then incorporate the egg yolk. Carefully mix in the flour, making sure not to over-work the dough (this stage is best done by hand). Pat the dough down into a greased baking tray to the thickness of a pound coin and bake for 15 mins or until lightly golden. Sprinkle with caster sugar and cut into rectangular pieces while still warm.

Cut 500g rhubarb into half centimetre dice and place in a large mixing bowl. Roughly chop the remaining 500g. Wrap the saffron, fennel seeds, vanilla pod and cinnamon in a piece of muslin cloth and secure with kitchen string. Place in a heavy-based pan with the rough-cut rhubarb, add the sugar, honey and cooking brandy and cook over a medium heat for 15-20 mins or until the rhubarb is a soft, stewed consistency.

Carefully remove the muslin bag of spices and discard, then strain the rhubarb through a sieve over the bowl of diced rhubarb, retaining the pulp. Leave to steep for 30 mins or until the diced rhubarb is soft but retains some bite. Refrigerate both the diced and reserved rhubarb pulp.

Serve the chilled lemon curd custards with a quenelle of each of the rhubarb compotes and two pieces of shortbread.

For the lemon curd custard

110g eggs
100g sugar
75ml lemon juice
½ leaf of gelatine (softened in cold water)
110g unsalted butter, cut into 1cm cubes
350g double cream

For the shortbread

200g butter
100g caster sugar, plus extra for sprinkling
1 egg yolk
250g plain flour

For the rhubarb compote

1kg rhubarb
pinch saffron
10 fennel seeds
½ vanilla pod
¼ cinnamon stick (or ¼ tsp powder)
325g sugar
30g honey
50ml cooking brandy

Bincho Yakitori

Preston Street has long been known as Brighton's restaurant row, but when you walk into Bincho Yakitori you're transported to a Tokyo back street. Chef David Miney's passion project is as close to an authentic izakaya - the Japanese equivalent of a gastropub - as you'll find in the UK.

Whenever the intimate, atmospheric restaurant is open, Miney is behind the counter tending the charcoal grill and sending out addictive plates of Teriyaki grilled quail, Grilled aubergine with miso and Crunchy karaage (Japanese fried chicken). You're also bound to see some off-duty chefs slaking their thirst on the excellent list of sake and Japanese craft beers.

"It's Japanese bar food - no frills, unfussy, ungarnished. It's all about the core ingredient. Yakitori means 'grilled bird' and it's key to what I do," says Miney (pictured right) who complements his menu of yakitori skewers and fried dishes with a specials board that might include Australian wagyu beef or Iberico pork, as well as some 'under the counter' items. "These may include chicken tail, gizzards and necks. I sell them to people in the know."

Although Miney has worked for the likes of Rick Stein in Cornwall and Simon Hopkinson at Bibendum in London, the three years he spent working in Tokyo inform the food at Bincho Yakitori. "It was tough. I wasn't getting paid but I was learning. I was like a sponge, writing everything down. The idea was to learn about kaiseki, the top end of Japanese fine dining, but while I was doing that I was spending a lot of time in yakatori joints and izakayas. That's when I thought, we've got to have something like this in the UK."

Bincho Yakitori originally opened in the Oxo Tower in London in 2007 and there were two further branches in Soho and Clerkenwell, but in 2015 Miney, who lives in the South Downs, decided to bring the concept a little closer to home.

He works closely with specialist suppliers to get obscure Japanese ingredients but some are more accessible. "Nama Yasai farm is just outside Lewes and I stop off on my way home on my motorbike to see what they've got. They grow things like Tokyo turnips, mitsuba greens, kinome herb and myoga shallots that I use to enhance dishes. People can't put their finger on the flavours, it's something they've never had before."

Bincho Yakitori

Grilled tenderstem broccoli with sesame and apple

(Serves 4)

Bonito flakes are available online and at Asian food outlets. Sprinkle them onto salads to add a wonderful smoky seasoning. You can substitute tahini for the Japanese sesame paste.

Blend all the sesame dressing ingredients together until smooth.

Blanch the broccoli in boiling water for 20 secs, then refresh in iced water. Drizzle lightly with sesame oil and grill on a barbecue or in a grill pan until lightly scorched.

To serve, cut the stems in half, place in the centre of four plates and spoon over some of the dressing. Top with the katsuobushi and scatter over the sesame seeds.

For the sesame dressing

100g Japanese sesame paste
1 Granny Smith apple, peeled and cored
250ml rapeseed oil
60ml rice wine vinegar
50ml mirin
30ml soy sauce
15ml dashi
5g sesame seeds
10g sesame oil, plus extra for grilling
50g white miso
40g chopped onion
10g grated ginger
10g grated garlic

To serve

500g tenderstem broccoli
4 tbsp bonito flakes (katsuobushi)
2 tbsp white sesame seeds
2 tbsp black sesame seeds

Grilled aubergine nasu with miso

(Serves 2)

This is far and away the most popular vegetarian dish on Bincho Yakitori's menu. The miso paste will last for several weeks in the fridge (without the egg) and can be used as an addition to sauces and dressings.

1 aubergine, cut in half lengthways
50-100ml vegetable oil
1 tbsp mixed black and white sesame seeds

For the miso sauce

250g sweet white miso (Saikyo miso works best)
80ml mirin
80ml sake
25g caster sugar
1 egg yolk

To make the sauce, put the miso, mirin, sake and sugar in a bowl, place over a pan of simmering water and whisk to amalgamate the ingredients. Cook gently for 45 mins, stirring regularly. Remove from the heat, allow to cool, then mix in the egg yolk.

Score the aubergine flesh with a sharp knife. Drizzle with oil, then grill on a barbecue on both sides until soft. If you don't have a barbecue, the aubergine can be cooked under an overhead grill, although the best results for the home cook are to shallow or deep-fry in a clean non-scented oil. You will be alarmed at how much oil they absorb - much of this will be expelled as it cooks - but quite frankly all great aubergine dishes need plenty of oil.

Allow the aubergine to cool slightly, then spread the miso on thickly - the back of a spoon works well for this.

Glaze under a hot grill or with a blow torch, sprinkle with sesame seeds and serve.

Crab, radish and wasabi salad

(Serves 4)

A fresh, light salad that's easy to make but looks impressive. If you can't find masago, a red caviar from the capelin fish, use salmon caviar.

2 egg yolks
½ tbsp rice wine vinegar
10g wasabi paste
1 tsp English mustard
5g cod roe
250ml vegetable oil
200g daikon, shredded
80g kohlrabi, shredded
240g white crab meat
20g nori, shredded
40g masago

Combine the egg yolks, vinegar, wasabi, mustard and roe in a large mixing bowl. Gradually whisk in the vegetable oil to make a wasabi mayonnaise.

Put the the daikon and kohlrabi in a bowl and stir in enough of the dressing to bind the salad ingredients lightly together.

Divide the salad between four serving plates, then scatter over some of the crab meat. Top with more of the salad and finish with a layer of crab meat. Scatter over the nori and masago and serve.

Japanese fried chicken (Kara age)

(Serves 2)

A dead easy Japanese take on fried chicken. double up on the recipe because this will be gone in a flash.

2 chicken legs
1 inch piece fresh ginger
6 tbsp sake
3 tbsp soy sauce
2 tbsp finely chopped spring onions
potato flour, for frying
3 litres vegetable oil (or enough to fill a deep-fat fryer or ¾ fill a large pan)

For the ponzu dipping sauce

4 tbsp soy sauce
4 tbsp lemon juice
4 tbsp rice vinegar

Bone the chicken legs and cut into bite-size pieces. Grate the ginger, place in a fine mesh sieve and push out the juice into a bowl using the back of a spoon. Add the sake, soy sauce, spring onions and chicken pieces and leave to marinate for 30 mins-1 hr.

To make the dipping sauce, combine the soy, lemon juice and vinegar in a bowl and stir well.

Heat a deep-fat fryer to 175°C. Remove the chicken from the bowl and toss in potato flour until coated liberally. Deep-fry until crisp and cooked through, then serve at once with the ponzu.

Slow cooked belly pork (Buta kakuni)

(Serves 4)

A signature of the restaurant, this pork is incredibly tender and delicious. The process of adding ginger and spring onion at the first stage of cooking will remove the strong meaty odour and prevents the meat tissue from breaking down, a practice always used in Japanese braised dishes.

Bring the water to a boil in a large saucepan and add the pork, then bring back to the boil and remove any impurities from the surface. Turn down to a simmer, add the sake, spring onions and ginger and cook very slowly for 2 hrs.

When the level of liquid comes just below the top of the meat, add the sugar and the mirin, then simmer again for 30 mins. Add the soy sauce and continue to cook for another 30 mins.

Boil the pak choi or greens, drain and cut into bite-size pieces. Arrange the pork on a serving dish with the greens and serve with the mustard and some steamed rice.

1.5 litres water
400g pork rib, cut into 5cm squares
120ml sake
2 spring onions
1 piece fresh ginger, peel only
50g caster sugar
120ml mirin
120ml soy sauce
2 heads of pak choi or greens of your choice
4 tbsp hot mustard, to serve
steamed rice, to serve

Soya milk doughnuts, hoji-cha ice cream

(Serves 6)

For the doughnuts

80g unsalted butter
100g caster sugar
200g plain flour
200g strong flour
4 tsp baking powder
3 eggs
100ml soya milk
zest 2 lemons
3 litres vegetable oil (or enough to fill a deep-fat
fryer or ¾ fill a large pan)
icing sugar, for dusting

For the ice cream

250ml double cream
250ml full-fat milk
100g caster sugar
6 large egg yolks
20g hoji-cha powder

Put all doughnut ingredients, apart from the icing sugar, into a
food processor and pulse to make a dough, being careful not
to overwork. Shape into a ball, wrap in cling film and put in the
fridge for 1 hr.

To make the ice cream, pour the cream and milk into a pan
and bring to a simmer. Whisk together the sugar and yolks in
a bowl. As soon as the creamy milk bubbles up the side of the
pan, remove from the heat and slowly trickle the liquid onto
the sugary yolks, beating well.

Pour the mixture into a clean heavy-based pan and stir over
low-to-medium heat until the mixture thickens and coats the
back of the spoon. Beat in the hoji-cha powder. Leave to cool
overnight. Pour the mixture into the bowl of an ice-cream
machine and churn until the ice cream is softly set. Transfer to
a freezer-proof container, cover and freeze until needed.

When ready to serve, heat a deep-fat fryer to 170°C. With
oiled hands, shape the dough into small balls about 4cm
diameter and deep-fry until golden. Remove from the fryer,
drain and dust with icing sugar. Serve with the ice cream.

This modern Indian brasserie reinvents sub-continental dining for the 21st century with its bright, contemporary interior, spicy cocktails and authentic regional dishes. Since its launch as a 40-seat bistro in the Lanes in 2008, and its continued success since 2011 when it moved to a much larger location within My Hotel in Jubilee Square, the restaurant has won numerous awards and accolades including four British Curry Awards, is listed in the National Restaurant Awards Top 100 in the country and is highly rated in the Hardens, AA and Michelin restaurant guides. But what really matters is the cracking service, buzzy atmosphere and unbeatable dishes like Kerala red duck curry and the Masala dosa.

"In the early days the food was very experimental - some of it worked and some of it didn't. We know who we are now and we're so much better and stronger in our identity," says chef Alun Sperring (pictured right) who owns and runs the restaurant with wife Dawn. "We've built a whole bunch of favourite dishes like momos and oxtail madras, things that we know customers really like."

Sperring studied for a City and Guilds qualification in catering at Brighton Tech (now City College) and his varied career includes cooking in Switzerland and Germany as well as a stint as head chef of a Moroccan restaurant in Dubai. But it was his time at the ground-breaking Cinnamon Club in London that turned out to be a life-changing experience.

"It really fuelled my thoughts that I could be part of the Indian cooking world. The style of cooking is quite alien, with the curries and the tandoor, and that's why not a lot of European chefs have Indian restaurants, because it's not an easy morph," says Sperring, who isn't afraid to mix up regional Indian traditions. "I might take a starch from one part of India and pair it with something from another region. I've had a few bust-ups with chefs, but for me it works."

Over the years, the Sperrings have gone from employing 12 staff to 50, and at the time of writing are about to make a crowdfunded leap to hiring many more, with a further four restaurants planned to open along the south coast. The future is undoubtedly hotting up for The Chilli Pickle.

The Chilli Pickle

Pork momos

(Serves 4)

Momos have been on The Chilli Pickle menu since day one - chef Alun Sperring calls them 'dim sum with attitude'. Although a Nepalese dish, you will find them all over India. At the restaurant, they're also served with a rib broth.

To make the filling, mix all the ingredients together in a bowl. Check the seasoning by frying off a small piece in a pan. Adjust if necessary and refrigerate for 1 hr. Form into small balls about 20-25g each and refrigerate while you make the wrappers.

In a bowl, mix the flour with the salt, then make a well in the middle. Pour in the water and mix well to form a dough. If the dough is too sticky, add a little more flour and if too dry add a little more water.

Knead the dough on a cool clean surface until smooth. Cover and refrigerate. Split the dough into 3 and roll into long cylinders around 2cm in diameter. Cut 1cm discs and roll each disc to a 5cm round.

Put a mince ball in the centre of each pastry disc and crimp the edges to seal. Place on a lightly floured tray to prevent sticking and repeat until all the pork and pastry is used. The momos can be frozen at this point.

For the sambhal, heat the oil in a pan and temper the cumin and garlic to a golden colour. Add the chilli flakes and cook for 1 min, being careful not to burn them. Add the chilli powder and a pinch of salt. Remove from the pan to prevent further cooking.

Steam the momos in a bamboo or perforated dim sum steamer for 10 mins (or 14 mins from frozen) and serve with the sambhal.

For the filling

400g pork shoulder, minced
100g white cabbage, finely sliced
1 banana shallot, finely diced
4 spring onions, finely sliced
75g cold butter, grated
25g smoked bacon, finely diced
½ tsp ground cumin
½ tsp coriander
½ tsp turmeric
½ tsp black pepper
2 green chillies, finely diced
1 tsp salt

For the wrappers

450g plain flour
½ tsp salt
180ml water

For the sambhal

120ml vegetable oil
1 dessertspoon cumin seeds
1 dessertspoon crushed garlic
1 dessertspoon chilli flakes
1 tsp Kashmiri chilli powder

Shellfish moily

(Serves 4)

This is a Chilli Pickle favourite that often returns to the menu. The crab cakes are coated in vermicelli to resemble sea urchin. Appam or soft fermented rice pancakes are great for mopping up the rich spicy sauce. You can buy packs of ready-to-make mix online.

For the crab cakes

100g white crab meat
100g brown crab meat
200g boiled potatoes, grated
1 pinch roasted cumin
1 tsp finely diced root ginger
1 dessertspoon chopped coriander
1 green chilli, finely diced
60g plain flour
2 eggs, beaten
1 pack Pakistani roasted vermicelli, crushed
3 litres vegetable oil (or enough to fill a deep-fat fryer or ¾ fill a large pan)

For the moily

2 dessertspoons extra virgin coconut oil
12 black peppercorns
2 star anise
1 cinnamon stick, 3cm long
4 cloves
½ tsp mustard seeds
1 shallot, finely sliced
2cm piece root ginger, cut into matchsticks
800ml coconut milk
½ tsp turmeric plus a pinch
2 green chillies, slit
16 curry leaves
1 dessertspoon lemon juice
8 scallops, shelled, cleaned and dried
1 tsp coconut oil
1 pinch salt
1 dessertspoon butter
1 tsp lemon juice
1kg mussels, cleaned, any open mussels discarded
100ml white wine

To make the crab cakes, mix the white and brown crab meat, potatoes, cumin, ginger, coriander and chilli in a bowl and season to taste. Form into small balls, about 20-25g each, and refrigerate. Place the flour in a bowl, the eggs in another and the crushed vermicelli in a third bowl. Coat the crab cake balls lightly in the flour, then the egg mix and lastly the vermicelli (this works best as a two-man job as it can get messy and you don't want the coating to become claggy).

To make the moily, heat a pan, add the coconut oil, black peppercorns, star anise, cinnamon stick, cloves and mustard seeds and cook for 1 min. Add the shallots and ginger and cook for 2 mins until lightly browned. Add the coconut milk and bring to a simmer, then add the ½ teaspoon of turmeric and green chillies and reduce by one quarter. Add the curry leaves and lemon juice and season to taste. Keep warm.

Mix the scallops in a bowl with the coconut oil, pinch of turmeric and salt. Heat a non-stick pan to very hot, then add the scallops and cook for 2 mins or until golden. Turn the scallops over and cook for 1 min. Add the butter and lemon juice and roll around the pan, then remove the scallops and buttery juices to a bowl ready to serve (the scallops will hold in the butter keeping them moist and warm).

Heat the oil in a deep-fat fryer to 180°C. Deep-fry the crab cakes for 2-3 mins or until golden and crisp.

Heat a large saucepan, pour in the mussels and wine, cover with a lid and steam for 2 mins or until most of the mussels have opened. Pour the hot moily sauce over the mussels, mix well and cook for 1-2 mins or until the remaining mussels have opened.

Portion the mussels into 4 bowls, top each bowl with 2 scallops, pour over any remaining sauce and top with 2 crab cakes. Serve with appam.

Barbecue red-spiced bream

(Serves 4)

In Kerala, pomfret is used for this dish and is available in the UK frozen, but with the sea on our doorstep, fresh sea bream is a more sensible choice. Its slightly more fatty, gelatinous texture keeps the fish moister and complements the fiery heat of the marinade.

4 x 400-500g sea bream, gutted and gills removed
100g Dutch long red chilli
1 lemongrass stick
5 lime leaves
½ tsp dried Arabic lime
30g root ginger
30g garlic cloves
½ tsp turmeric powder
1 tbsp vegetable oil
125ml thick yoghurt

For the coconut congee

250g basmati rice
500ml water
4 green cardamom pods, crushed
400ml coconut milk
1 tsp finely diced root ginger

With a sharp knife, cut incisions 2cm apart along both sides of the bream. In a pestle and mortar, grind the chilli, lemongrass, lime leaves, dried lime, ginger and garlic to a paste. Mix with the turmeric, oil and yoghurt and add a large pinch of salt. Rub 1 tbsp of the marinade over each fish, inside and out. Refrigerate for a minimum of 2 hrs.

To make the congee, put the rice, water and cardamom pods in a pan and bring to a simmer. Cook until the rice is very soft. Add the coconut milk and continue cooking to a light porridge. Stir in the ginger and season with a large pinch of salt and cracked black pepper.

Cook the fish on a barbecue for 15 mins or until cooked through. The marinade will add to the smoke but if you want to completely avoid this, wrap the fish in tin foil and place the whole parcel on the barbecue. Alternatively, you can bake the bream in the oven, but you won't get the same smoky barbecue flavour. Divide the congee between 4 bowls and serve with the fish.

The feast of pork that won The Chilli Pickle the title of
Best OctoberBEST dish 2017, recipe overleaf

Pork knuckle vindaloo

(Serves 8)

Alun Sperring spent two years in Munich as a young man and consumed many a Schweinshaxe (roasted pork knuckle) in beer gardens and at the Oktoberfest. This is his Indian-style tribute to those days. The wrap-around blanket of crackling makes the dish a real showstopper when brought to the table.

Heat oven to 200°C. Put the sliced onions and potatoes in a roasting tin. Mix the turmeric, salt and oil in a small bowl, then rub evenly over the knuckles. Put the knuckles on top of the potatoes and onions, making sure there is space between each knuckle to allow for even cooking. Pour water into the roasting tin about 2.5cm deep, then roast in the oven for 10 mins. Open the oven door to cool slightly and reduce the temperature to 150°C. Top up the water to 2.5cm, baste the pork and cook for 1 hr. Baste again and cook for 1 hr more.

Take pork out of the oven and increase the temperature to 265°C. Pour the beer over the knuckles and return to the oven for 4-5 mins or until the skin is fully blistered and crackling. Save any liquor in the tray for vindaloo gravy - there should be about 250ml.

While the pork is cooking, begin making the gravy by dry-roasting the peppercorns, cloves, cinnamon stick and cumin seeds until lightly smoked and fragrant. Cool and grind with the whole dried chillies to a fine powder. Add the tomato paste and vinegar and grind to a paste.

Heat the vegetable oil in a pan and cook the diced onion and garlic until dark golden in colour, stirring regularly to prevent burning. Add the tomatoes and cook until the liquid is reduced. Add the blended spice paste and cook for 1 min. Add the chicken stock, bring to a simmer and reduce by a quarter. Add the jaggery, pork roasting juices and 2 halves of habanero chilli. Simmer for 2 mins, then remove the chilli and check the seasoning.

Serve 1 knuckle between two people with some of the gravy. At the restaurant, the knuckles come with naan bread, spicy potatoes, pickles and raita.

2 onions, thickly sliced
2 potatoes, thickly sliced
1 tsp turmeric
½ tbsp salt
3 tbsp vegetable oil
4 pork knuckles
1 bottle of beer of your choice

For the vindaloo gravy

20 black peppercorns
15 cloves
10g cinnamon stick
10g cumin seeds
10 dried whole red chillies
40g tomato paste
75ml malt vinegar
100ml vegetable oil
200g white onions, finely diced
25g garlic, crushed
300g ripe red tomatoes, diced
500ml chicken stock
15g jaggery
1 habanero chilli, halved

Pistachio kulfi and gulab jaman

(Serves 4)

Kulfi is a set Indian ice cream and very different from the churned Western style. Rich and full flavoured, its dense fudgy texture is created by the reduction of milk and cream, but this easier version achieves the same effect with condensed milk. Kulfi moulds are available online.

For the pistachio kulfi

250g unsalted peeled pistachios, plus extra to serve
100ml water
50g sugar
400ml condensed milk
400ml evaporated milk
400ml double cream

For the gulab jaman

200g milk powder
110g plain flour
1 tsp baking powder
½ tsp bicarbonate of soda
350ml full-fat milk
25g ghee or clarified butter, melted
3 litres vegetable oil (or enough to fill a deep-fat fryer or ¾ fill a large pan)
200g caster sugar
25ml rose water
2 cardamom pods
100ml water

Heat oven to 180°C. Roast all of the pistachio nuts on a baking tray for 8 mins. Leave to cool, reserve a few to serve, then finely grind 250g. Boil the water and sugar, then stir in the ground nuts to make a smooth paste. Remove from the heat and allow to cool (this makes far more paste than you'll need for this recipe, but it can be used in many other desserts).

Blend the condensed milk, evaporated milk, double cream and 2 dessertspoons of the pistachio paste together. Pour into kulfi moulds and freeze.

To make the gulab jaman, mix the milk powder, flour, baking powder, bicarb, milk and ghee or butter together in a bowl and add enough water to create a soft dough. Do not overwork or they will become dense. Cover and leave for 10 mins in a cool place. Heat the oil in a deep-fat fryer to 170°C. Form the dough into smooth, marble-size balls, then deep fry until golden. Drain on kitchen paper and allow to cool.

Heat the sugar, rose water and cardamom pods in the water to create a syrup. Remove from the heat, add the gulab jaman to the syrup and leave to soak for a minimum of 2 hrs.

To serve, heat the gulab jaman in the syrup in the microwave for 30 secs or until warmed through. Be careful not to heat them for too long or they will implode and lose their lightness. Serve with pistachio kulfi, a sprinkling of roasted crushed pistachios and some of the syrup spooned around.

The Little Fish Market

Tucked away on a side street just off Hove seafront, Surrey-born chef Duncan Ray (pictured right) cooks some of the best modern seafood dishes in the country. A favourite haunt of Brighton's off-duty chefs (many of whom reckon Little Fish Market deserves a Michelin star), this intimate 20-cover double-aspect dining room, overseen by Rob Smith who runs front-of-house solo with exceptional charm and efficiency, has been simply but stylishly transformed from its previous incarnation as a fishmonger's shop with seafood-themed drawings, wooden tables and comfortably upholstered chairs.

"I knew I wanted to cook on my own so that the food at the restaurant was consistent, and fish lends itself to that set up. It cooks faster, meaning I've got time to prepare starters and desserts," says Ray. "There was a big gap of really good restaurants along the coastline between Kent and Dorset. I've always loved Brighton and, being by the sea, I just thought a fish restaurant would suit."

During the mid to late 90s, Ray worked in some of the best kitchens in Europe including L'Ortolan, Lettonie, The Fat Duck and the three-Michelin starred Georges Blanc in eastern France. After several years travelling, he returned to the UK at the age of 23 to take the head chef role at Penny Hill Park Hotel before spending six years as a private chef, cooking for A-listers and royalty. He then ran The Five Alls in the Cotswolds before opening Little Fish Market in 2013.

Early à la carte menus included Ray's personal twists on classics like fish and chips, and what have become perennial favourites such as Monkfish and pork belly with carrot and star anise purée. Over time, his food has evolved to incorporate highly sophisticated creations like Salmagundi - a seasonally changing signature dish made (in spring) with sea trout, asparagus, caramelised and raw cauliflower, raw long radish, poached Romanesco, Jersey Royals, tempura courgette flower, watercress, keta caviar and kiwi – a multitude of textures and temperatures.

"The last four years have been the most influential of my life. I've learnt more about food and have more of an understanding of everything I've been taught than ever before," he says. "I want to cook good food that people want to eat. The famous chef Nico Ladenis always said 'Precision, restraint and simplicity' - and that's what I live my life by."

The Little Fish Market

Loch Duart salmon, posh potato salad, fennel

(Serves 4)

Loch Duart salmon is a high-quality, sustainably-farmed fish and worth paying a little bit extra for. If you can't find Ratte potatoes, substitute another waxy variety such as Charlotte.

4 skinless salmon fillets (200g each)
250g Ratte potatoes, cut into 1.5cm dice
2 tbsp mayonnaise
zest 1 unwaxed lemon
1 tsp finely chopped chives
1 fennel bulb, finely sliced
juice 1 orange
1 tbsp fennel seeds, soaked in water overnight
1 litre rapeseed oil

Trim the salmon fillets and remove any bones. Cook the potato in salted water for around 5 mins or until tender, then cool under cold running water. Mix together the mayonnaise, lemon zest and chives, add enough of the mix to the potato to bind and season to taste. Dress the fennel slices with the orange juice, fennel seeds and a little salt.

Gently heat the rapeseed oil in a saucepan to 50°C (check with a heat probe), ensuring that there is enough oil to submerge the salmon. Add the salmon, then remove the pan from the heat. Leave the fish to cook for 5-7 mins or until a skewer passes easily through it.

To serve, divide the dressed fennel between four plates, top with the salmon and arrange the potato salad around the plate.

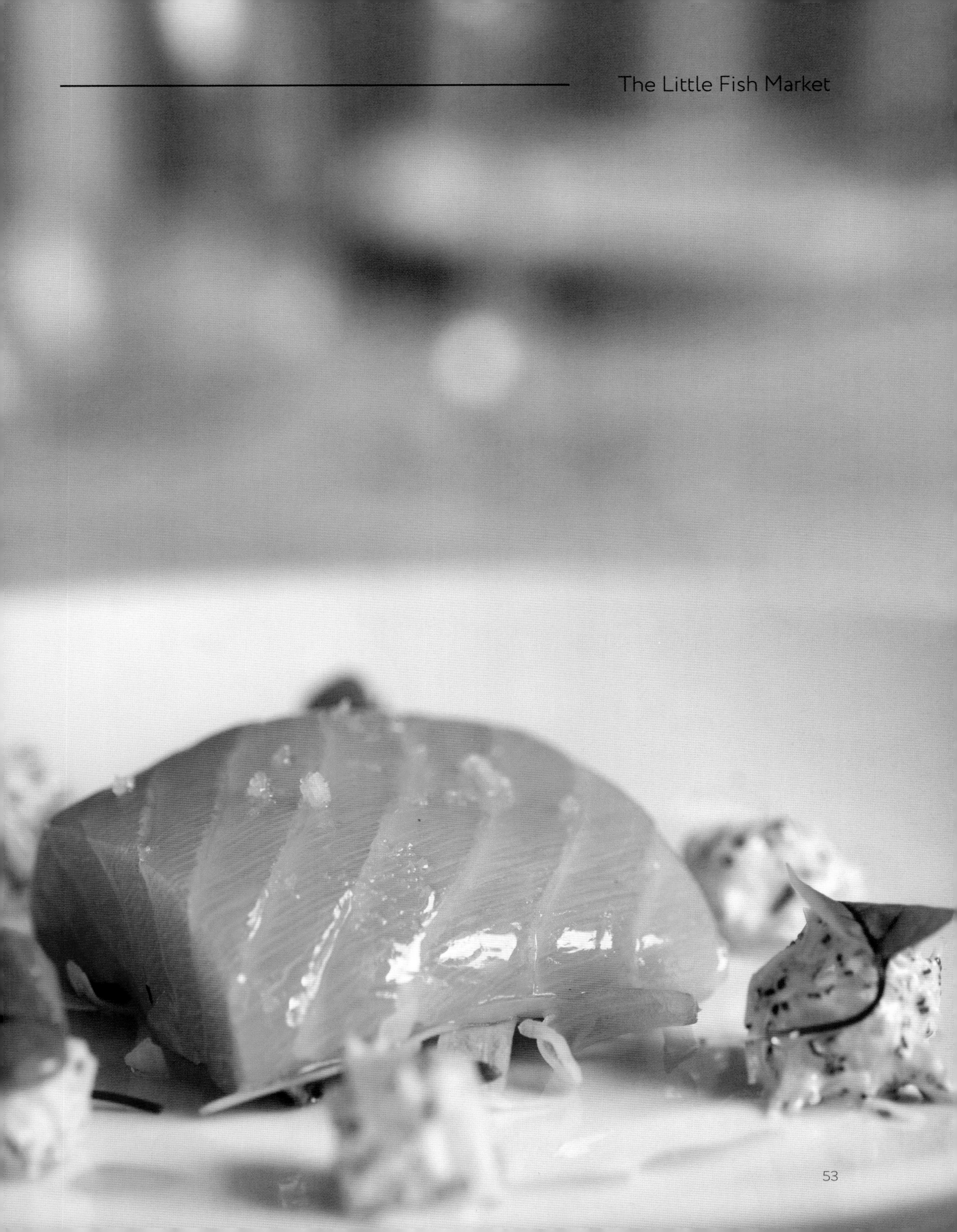

Skrei cod, potato purée, brown shrimp, brown butter

(Serves 4)

Skrei is a line-caught Norwegian migratory cod variety with firm white flesh that's rich in vitamins and minerals and is now available from some supermarkets. If you can't find it, just substitute any other variety of cod.

Skin the cod fillets and trim to a neat shape. Put the potatoes in a pan and cover with water. Bring to the boil, add 1 tsp salt and simmer until tender. Meanwhile, heat the milk. Drain the potatoes and mash until smooth, beat in 30g of the butter then stir in the hot milk. Season and keep warm.

Season the cod fillets with a little salt and put into a medium-hot frying pan with the oil. Cook for a couple of mins, depending on the thickness of the fillet. The fish is cooked when you can pass a skewer through the flesh with no resistance.

Mix together the brown shrimps, cucumber, parsley, spring onion and capers in a heatproof bowl and set aside. Put the remaining 100g butter into a pan and bring rapidly the boil until it foams and starts to brown. Quickly add the lemon juice (it will spit but this is normal). Pour the butter mix over the brown shrimp mix to make a sauce.

To serve, divide the mash between four plates, top with a fillet of cod and spoon over some of the sauce.

4 Skrei cod fillets (200g each)
400g Maris Piper potatoes, diced
30ml milk
130g salted butter
1 tbsp rapeseed oil
100g brown shrimps, peeled
½ cucumber, diced
10g chopped parsley
2 spring onions, sliced
25g small capers
juice 1 lemon

Line-caught bass, brandade stuffed piquillo pepper, Umbrian lentils

(Serves 4)

This is an elegant and richly delicious dish. You can buy salt cod and piquillo peppers at the supermarket but you may have to source the Umbrian lentils from an online supplier, although puy lentils are widely available. The brandade is wonderful on its own served with crusty white bread or on croutons for a dinner party.

Trim the bass and check for pin bones by running your finger down the centre of the fillet and removing with tweezers. Put the salt cod in a pan, cover with milk and add the garlic, thyme and bay. Bring to the boil, then remove from the heat. The cod should be cooked - if not leave it in the milk for 1 min more, then remove and allow to cool.

Put the diced potatoes in a pan and cover with water. Bring to the boil, add ½ tsp salt and simmer until tender. Drain and mash until smooth.

Make the brandade by heating the olive oil in a wide bottomed pan and flaking in the cooked cod, stirring constantly until the oil is incorporated into the fish. Transfer to a food mixer and beat on the highest speed. The cod should become white. Reduce the speed and add the potato followed by the cream and the chopped parsley. Taste and adjust the seasoning, then allow to cool.

Stuff the peppers with the brandade and refrigerate until needed.

Put the lentils in a pan, cover with water and bring to the boil. Add ½ tsp salt and simmer until tender. Drain and allow to cool.

Heat oven to 200°C. Put the brandade-stuffed pepper in the oven to warm for 5 mins. Reheat the lentils in the butter and 100ml water. Heat the oil in a non-stick frying pan over a medium heat and cook the bass skin-side down for a few mins. Turn the fillets over and remove from the heat. The fish is cooked when a skewer passes through the flesh without resistance.

To serve, mound the lentils onto four plates, top each with a bass fillet and place a stuffed pepper pointing upwards on each plate. At the restaurant, the dish is garnished with a potato crisp, 10-year-old balsamic and deep-fried parsley.

4 wild bass fillets (200g each)
100g salt cod
300ml milk
1 garlic clove
1 thyme sprig
1 bay leaf
200g Maris Piper potatoes, diced
100ml olive oil
50g double cream
1 tbsp chopped parsley
280g jar piquillo pepper, drained and deseeded
200g Umbrian lentils or puy lentils
25g butter
1 tbsp rapeseed oil

Turbot, roast chicken, sherry, morels

(Serves 4)

This is a truly luxurious dish that utilises some of the finest products from the sea, forest and vineyard. Turbot, morels and Sauternes don't come cheap so save this for a special occasion. Fresh morels only have a short season in April and May so substitute the dried version (rehydrated) or quartered chestnut mushrooms the rest of the year.

4 skinless turbot fillets, boned (150g each)
250ml water
125g unsalted butter
4 organic chicken wings
1 tsp rapeseed oil

For the sauce

100ml sherry
100ml Sauternes dessert wine
200ml fish stock
200ml double cream
20 fresh morel mushrooms, washed and halved lengthwise

4 whole spring onions
1 head hispi cabbage, shredded
50g samphire, salty fingers or sea aster

Heat oven to 200°C. Put the turbot in a heatproof dish with 150ml of the water and 100g of the butter. Season, cover with buttered baking parchment and set aside. Toss the chicken wings in the oil, season and roast for 15 mins or until brown and cooked through. Leave the oven on while you make the sauce.

Put the sherry and Sauternes in a pan and reduce over a high heat to a syrup. Add the stock and reduce further to about 100ml. Add the cream and reduce again until you have about 200ml sauce. Add the morels and heat through for several mins. Season to taste.

Season the spring onions, then grill for 1 min on each side until cooked and lightly charred.

Bake the turbot for 4-7 mins depending on how thick the fillet is. The fish is cooked when a skewer passes easily through the flesh without resistance.

Put the cabbage in a pan with the remaining 25g butter and 100ml water, and cook for 2 mins. Drain and season. Boil whichever sea vegetable you are using for 1 min, then drain and season.

Divide the cabbage, spring onion and sea vegetables between four plates and top with the turbot. Place a chicken wing on each plate and spoon over the sauce (there should be 10 morel halves per plate).

Nougat glace, passionfruit, chocolate

(Makes 12)

This is a great dish for a large dinner party as everything is done in advance. As it's frozen, it keeps well if you're serving smaller numbers, too. You'll find passionfruit purée online, or substitute a good-quality shop-bought sorbet.

405g caster sugar
125g hazelnuts
120g egg whites
100ml double cream
20g glucose
50ml water
15g cocoa powder
500ml passionfruit purée

To make the hazelnut praline, gently heat 225g of the caster sugar in a heavy-based pan over a medium heat to make a caramel. Add the hazelnuts and cook for 2 mins, carefully swirling the pan (avoid splashing the caramel as it will burn if it comes into contact with skin) until caramelised and brown. Pour onto a baking tray lined with baking paper and leave to cool. Break the praline into very small pieces using a rolling pin or hammer and set aside.

In a stand mixer, make a meringue by whisking the egg whites for 1 min. Continue to whisk while gradually adding 80g sugar until the mixture forms stiff peaks. In a separate bowl, whisk the cream to soft peaks. Fold the meringue into the whipped cream until incorporated, then fold in the crushed praline to finish the nougat glace. Spoon the mixture into twelve 30 x 80 x 30mm silicone moulds and freeze for at least 2 hrs or until set.

Make the chocolate sauce by putting the glucose and remaining 100g sugar in a pan and cooking over a medium-low heat to a light-coloured caramel. Stir in the water and cocoa powder, then strain and set aside.

Churn the passionfruit purée in an ice-cream maker until set, then freeze until needed.

To serve, de-mould each nougat glace onto a plate, add a scoop of sorbet and some of the chocolate sauce.

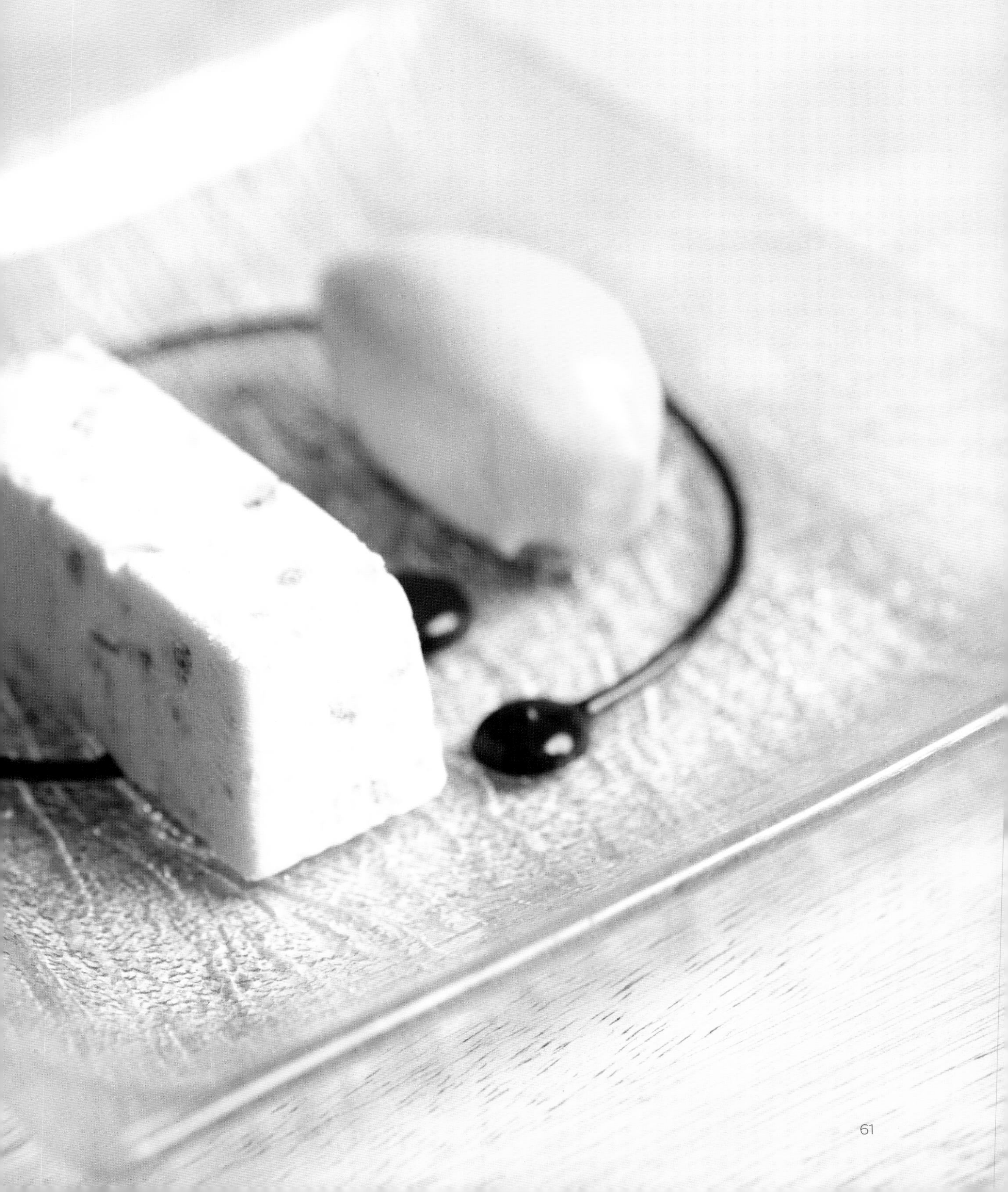

Located within The Artist Residence boutique hotel that occupies two 19th century townhouses in Brighton's Regency Square, The Set fuses the city's elegant Regency past with its Bohemia-chic present. Exposed brick, rustic wood tables, reclaimed doors and neon signs create a relaxed contemporary environment for the modern seasonal British cooking of Dan Kenny (pictured right). Sit at the counter overlooking the 20-seater restaurant's open kitchen to see the chefs prepare signature dishes like Carrot tartare or enjoy small plates such as Beef cheek hash.

"The Set was a complete accident, a bolt out of the blue," says Shropshire-born Kenny who arrived in Brighton after living in Ho Chi Minh City for two years, where he studied Vietnamese cuisine. He landed a job at The Gingerman where he met Brigihgton-native Semone Bonner who had previously worked at the late lamented One Paston Place, Hotel Du Vin and Grand Hotel before spending two years in France.

"We liked working together. We had very different styles but we liked each other's food," says Kenny, who launched The Set as a pop-up with Bonner in 2014. "We did a Halloween dinner at The Artist Residence and met the owners. They tried a few dishes, then called us about a week later and asked if we wanted to open a restaurant."

By March 2015, The Set was up and running and came to the attention of the national press, restaurant guides and food bloggers, although Kenny admits to 'cringing' at some of the early menus which he puts down to a rushed opening and keenness to impress. "We've matured. We still try to keep it inventive with combinations, but the ethos is to get clarity of flavour out of fewer ingredients."

Now run solely by Kenny (Bonner left the restaurant in 2017 to pursue other projects), The Set is the epitome of a modern, forward-thinking restaurant. But when it comes to developing new dishes, there's no culinary laboratory. "I just go for a pint with a list of ingredients. I call our suppliers from the pub and ask them what's good."

The Set

In 2016, Kenny branched out, opening Dizzy Gull at the nearby Brighton Beer Dispensary serving 'food for drunk people' as well as a stellar Sunday lunch. Whatever comes next is set to be another success.

The Set

Chicken nuggets, red cabbage ketchup

(Makes 20-25 nuggets)

This snack has been on and off the menu since The Set first opened and is inspired by its famous fast-food cousin and nostalgic, endearing quality. The ketchup changes through the seasons dependent on the vegetables available.

First make the stock. Put the wings, carcass and water into a large pan and bring to a simmer. Skim all impurities and fat off the top with a ladle and discard. Add the celery, onion, carrot, leek and garlic. Wrap the peppercorns, thyme, star anise, bay and salt in a muslin and tie with kitchen string to secure. Simmer for 4 hrs, skimming any impurities every 45 mins.

Add the chicken legs to the stock, cover and cook for 20 mins on a very low simmer. Remove from the heat and leave the legs to gently poach in the stock for a further 30 mins. Remove and allow to cool.

In a medium pan on a low heat, cook the diced shallot and garlic in the butter for 10 mins or until translucent but not coloured. Remove from the heat, add the tarragon, sage, rosemary and thyme and allow to cool. Shred the chicken legs into a large mixing bowl. Add the shallot and herb mix along with the olive oil, mustard and sherry vinegar. Mix well and season to taste with salt and a splash more vinegar if required. Roll into small nugget-sized pieces and refrigerate for 1 hr to firm up.

Set out three containers: one with the flour, one with the milk and eggs whisked together and one with breadcrumbs. A few at a time, pass the nuggets first through the flour, then the milk and egg mix and finally the breadcrumbs, making sure they are well coated during each process. Return to the fridge while you make the ketchup.

Put all of the ketchup ingredients into a large pan with a pinch of salt, cover and simmer for 90 mins. Remove from the heat and, while still hot, blend until smooth. Adjust the seasoning and allow to cool.

To serve, heat the oil in a deep-fat fryer to 180°C. Deep-fry the nuggets in batches until golden-brown and serve with the ketchup.

For the chicken stock

8 chicken wings
1 chicken carcass
4 litres water
1 celery stick, roughly chopped
1 onion, roughly chopped
1 carrot, roughly chopped
1 leek, roughly chopped
6 garlic cloves
5 white peppercorns
1 thyme sprig
1 star anise
1 bay leaf
2 tbsp kosher salt

For the chicken nugget mix

5 chicken legs
4 shallots, diced
4 garlic cloves
100g butter
1 tsp finely chopped tarragon
1 tsp finely chopped sage
1 tsp finely chopped rosemary
1 tsp finely chopped thyme
1 tbsp olive oil
1 tbsp Dijon mustard
2 tbsp sherry vinegar
200g flour
200ml milk
2 eggs
200g panko breadcrumbs
3 litres vegetable oil (or enough to fill a deep fat fryer or ¾ fill a large pan)

For the red cabbage ketchup

1 small red cabbage, core removed and leaves thinly sliced
2 shallots
2 garlic cloves
1 bay leaf
1 tbsp yellow mustard seeds
2 tbsp English mustard
1 star anise
50ml apple cider vinegar
50 ml red wine vinegar
500ml chicken stock
150g brown sugar

Carrot tartare

(Serves 4)

This is one of the most popular dishes at The Set where starters on the four-course menu are always vegetarian. The beef in a classic tartare has been swapped for black carrots, which retain the punchy, meaty flavour and texture of the original.

10 black carrots
1 shallot, finely diced
1 tbsp lilliput capers, finely diced
1 tbsp finely chopped parsley
5 cornichons, finely diced
1 tsp finely chopped tarragon
50g Parmesan, finely grated, plus extra to serve

For the dressing

50ml olive oil
50ml rapeseed oil
1 tsp Tabasco
1 tsp Maldon sea salt
1 tsp Dijon mustard
1 tsp tomato ketchup

10 egg yolks
300ml white balsamic vinegar
1 tsp salt
100g butter
2 slices focaccia, diced into 1cm cubes
3 litres vegetable oil (or enough to fill a deep-fat fryer or ¾ fill a large pan)

Peel and finely grate eight of the carrots and mix together in a bowl with the shallot, capers, parsley, cornichons, tarragon and Parmesan. Make the dressing by putting the oils, Tabasco, salt, mustard and ketchup in a plastic bottle and shaking until amalgamated. Alternatively, whisk together in a bowl. Dress the carrot mix until well coated.

To make the egg yolk purée, poach the yolks in salted boiling water for 1 min, remove and place in a bowl of iced water to cool. Blend with a pinch of salt until smooth, transfer to a piping bag and refrigerate.

To make pickled carrots, bring the balsamic vinegar and salt to the boil in a small pan. Finely slice one carrot on a mandolin, place in a bowl and pour over the warm balsamic. Now make the croutons. Heat the butter in a frying pan until golden, add the diced bread and fry until golden-brown.

To make carrot crisps, heat the oil in a deep-fat fryer or large pan to 160°C. Peel the remaining carrot and cut into long strips with a vegetable peeler. Deep-fry until the carrot is silent in the fryer - this indicates all of its moisture has gone. Drain on kitchen paper and season.

To serve, divide the dressed carrots between 4 plates, making a small well in the centre of each. Pipe an egg yolk-sized amount of the purée into the well, arrange pickled carrots around the carrot mix and generously grate Parmesan over the entire dish. Scatter over the croutons and carrot crisps and serve immediately.

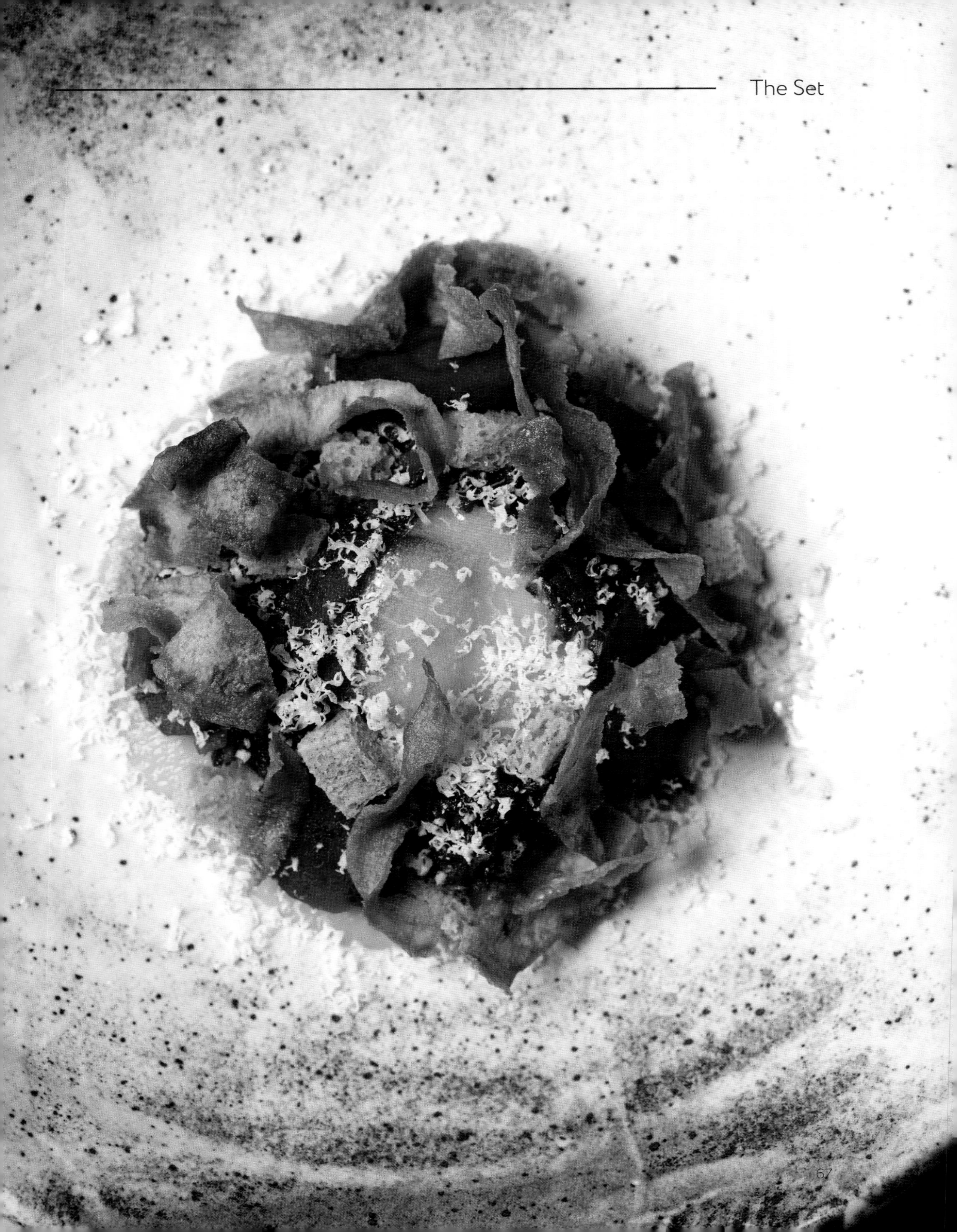

A comforting yet elegant beef dish from The Set

1 tbsp black treacle
2 beef cheeks
1 tbsp butter
1 onion, roughly chopped
1 carrot, roughly chopped
1 fennel, roughly chopped
1 garlic bulb, halved
500ml red wine
1 tbsp Marmite
1 thyme sprig
1 rosemary sprig
2 litres beef stock

For the parsley and tarragon crumb

25g parsley
5g tarragon
80g spinach
100g flour
30g butter
80g water
5g truffle oil
1 black peppercorn

For the deep-fried Marmite mash

300g Maris Piper potatoes, diced
150ml water
50g butter
90g plain flour
2 eggs
1 tsp Marmite
3 litres vegetable oil (or enough to fill a deep-fat
fryer or ¾ fill a large pan)

For the turnips and radishes

100g golden syrup
100g Marmite
1 tsp butter
2 white turnips, diced
2 watermelon turnips, diced
10 breakfast radishes, diced
1 small bunch parsley, roughly chopped

Beef cheek, marmite mash, turnip

(Serves 4)

This is a very rich dish that's as satisfying to cook as it is to eat - brining, marinating and slowly braising meat for a long time is more rewarding than simply searing a lean cut. Ideal for winter, the dish can be served all year round - just choose some seasonal vegetables to accompany it.

Heat oven to 180°C. Rub the treacle evenly into the beef cheeks, then fry in the butter in a large pan until browned on all sides. Remove, then in the same pan, caramelise the onion, carrot, fennel and garlic for 10-15 mins. Add the wine, Marmite and herbs and reduce to a light syrup consistency. Add the beef stock, bring to a simmer and put the cheeks back in the pan. Cover with foil and braise in the oven for 2 hrs or until tender but not falling apart.

Remove the cheeks from pan and allow to cool. Strain the stock through a fine sieve into a clean pan and reduce by half over a high heat, skimming any impurities that rise to the surface with a ladle. Check for seasoning and consistency - the sauce should coat the back of a spoon and be clear and shiny.

Once the cheeks have cooled, pull them to pieces into a bowl and season. Add 100ml of the beef sauce, then spoon the beef mixture onto cling film and roll into a sausage. Refrigerate until totally cool, then cut the rolled cheek into 4 equal portions. Pan fry, still wrapped in the cling film, until browned on both the exposed sides - this should take about 8 mins in total.

To make the crumb, blanch the parsley, tarragon and spinach for a couple of seconds, refresh in iced water and squeeze dry. Blend with the flour, butter, water, truffle oil and peppercorn until smooth. Pour into a cream whipper, charge three times, then rest the mix for 30 mins. Squirt the crumb mix into a small paper cup and microwave for 30 secs to make a sponge. Tear the sponge into small pieces and place in a dehydrator or low oven until completely dry. Process to a crumb in a blender or with your hands, then store in an airtight container.

To make the deep-fried mash, boil the potatoes in salted water until soft, then mash and allow to cool. Meanwhile, simmer the 150ml water and butter in a pan. Gradually add the flour and cook for 10 mins, stirring constantly. Remove from the heat and add one egg at a time, whisking constantly until the mix has a dropping consistency. Allow to cool, then combine well with the potato and stir in the Marmite. Heat the oil in a deep-fat fryer to 190°C, then deep-fry teaspoons of the mix for 3 mins each or until puffed and golden brown.

To cook the veg, melt the golden syrup and Marmite in a pan, stirring continuously, then allow to cool. Heat 1 tsp butter in a pan and fry the turnips and radishes for 2-3 mins or until they just start to colour. Add 1 tbsp of the Marmite glaze and a big pinch of parsley. Cook for a further min until the turnips and radishes are nicely glazed and sticky.

To serve, place a piece of beef in the centre of 4 plates and sprinkle some crumb over the top. Spoon the glazed turnips and radishes around, then top with three pieces of the fried mash. Spoon over a tablespoon of the sauce and serve immediately.

The Set transform blood orange into a visually stunning and delicate dessert, recipe overleaf

For the blood orange gel, jelly and granita

2.35 litres fresh blood orange juice
5g agar agar
oil, for greasing
6 leaves soaked gelatine

For the blood orange sorbet

1 blood orange, zested then peeled and
segmented
1 tbsp glucose
100g brown sugar

For the caramelised white chocolate and
aerated chocolate

650g white chocolate, chopped
50ml rapeseed oil

For the white chocolate cookies

125g soft butter
100g brown sugar
100g caster sugar
1 egg
250g self-raising flour
pinch salt
30g white chocolate, chopped

Blood orange, white chocolate, cookie

(Serves 4)

It's always a pleasure when blood oranges are in season. They taste and look so good, plus there's not much else kicking about at the start of the year. Here, we use this beautiful fruit in lots of different ways.

Make the blood orange gel. Bring 500ml of the juice to a simmer in a pan. Add the agar agar and whisk constantly for 3 mins. Remove from the heat and strain through a fine sieve into a container. Allow to cool to room temperature, then set in the fridge for 1 hr or until it resembles very hard, rigid set jelly. Blend this jelly for 2 mins or to a smooth gel-like texture, then pour it into a plastic squeezy bottle or sealed container.

Make the blood orange jelly. Oil a small tub or mould and line with cling film, making sure there are no air bubbles. Soak the gelatine in water for 10 mins, drain and squeeze out any excess liquid. Heat 100ml blood orange juice in a pan until warm, add the gelatine and whisk to amalgamate. Add another 400ml juice and whisk well. Strain through a fine sieve into the lined tub or mould and leave for 4-5 hrs or overnight to set.

To make the blood orange sorbet, heat 1 litre blood orange juice with half the orange zest, the glucose and brown sugar in a pan. Strain through a fine sieve and allow to cool. Churn in an ice-cream machine and freeze until needed.

Make a granita by freezing the remaining 350ml blood orange juice in a small tub. Freeze overnight until solid.

To make caramelised white chocolate, heat oven to 120°C. Put 400g white chocolate on a small baking tray or in a heatproof dish and bake for 1 hr, stirring every 15 mins until it becomes thick and light caramel in colour. Pour the chocolate onto a large piece of baking parchment and spread as thinly as you can with a palette knife. Once cool, refrigerate for 1 hr (you may need to cut the parchment in half or quarters to fit it in the fridge). Break the chocolate into shards (it should have a snap to it and resemble Caramac). Store in-between sheets of parchment in a sealed tub.

To make aerated white chocolate, line a small container or mould with cling film and put it in the freezer. Melt the remaining 250g white chocolate with the oil in a bain marie until smooth and shiny. Pour into a cream whipper with a charge with a gas capsule. Shake vigorously for 2 mins, then repeat the process with a second capsule. Squirt the mix into the frozen tub and return to the freezer

Make white chocolate cookies. Heat oven to 180°C. Cream the butter and both sugars together for 10 mins until light, pale and fluffy (this is best done in a stand mixer). Whisk the egg and slowly beat into the creamed mix, followed by the flour and salt.

Fold in the chocolate chips and set in the fridge for 1 hr. Roll into small balls and place on a baking sheet lined with a non-stick matt or baking parchment. Bake for 6 mins, turn over and cook for a further 2 mins or until light golden-brown and soft and chewy in the middle. Allow to cool slightly, then cool on a rack.

To serve, place a rectangle of the jelly on each plate that's been chilled in the freezer. Put a dollop of blood orange gel next to the jelly, break a cookie into a few pieces and crumble over the top. Place a large shard or two of the caramelised white chocolate on the side of the jelly. Place a few segments of blood orange in and around the jelly. Put a scoop of sorbet on the gel to keep it in place. Scrape the frozen blood orange to a granita with a fork and scatter over the top of the dessert to finish.

Cereal milk

(Serves 6)

This is a signature dish at The Set. You will need a dehydrator to make the milk foam but they are relatively inexpensive and a useful bit of kit to have in your kitchen (though the recipe still works well without foam). For a more simple preparation, just top the panna cotta with chocolate, fruit and berries.

For the panna cotta and milk foam

2 litres full-fat milk
500ml cream
150g Cheerios or cereal of your choice
150g Crunchy Nut Cornflakes or cereal of your choice
6 gelatine leaves
125g caster sugar
6 tbsp glucose

For the sugar puffs

200g spelt
100g icing sugar
1 litre rapeseed oil

For the milk ice cream

50ml semi-skimmed milk
400g condensed milk

For the granola

100g puffed rice
100g oats
50g honey
1 tbsp glucose
50g butter.

Pour 500ml of the milk into a large container. Add the cream and cereals and allow to infuse for a minimum of 4 hrs or overnight in the fridge. Strain into a clean container, discarding the cereal.

Soften the gelatine leaves in cold water for 10 mins. Put the creamy cereal-infused milk in a pan, add the sugar and heat gently. Squeeze the excess water from the gelatine and add to the hot milk, stirring carefully to ensure you don't create any bubbles. Divide the milk evenly between 6 cereal bowls and set in the fridge for 4 hrs. When set, it should have a slight wobble but won't set hard.

Make a milk foam by first lining a dehydrator tray with parchment. Put 500ml full-fat milk into a pan with 5 tbsp glucose and bring very gently to a simmer, whisking constantly. Remove from the heat and blitz with a hand blender for 30 secs. Allow to rest for a further 30 secs, then skim off the foam with a ladle and place on the prepared tray. Repeat the process until the milk will no longer foam.

Dehydrate for 8 hrs at 90°C until the milk is crisp. Break into large shards and store in an airtight container.

Make the 'sugar puffs' by rinsing the spelt under a cold tap for 5 mins. Bring to the boil in a pan of water and cook for 20-25 mins or until the individual grains are plump and softened. Meanwhile, heat oven to 100°C. Drain the spelt, cool under a cold tap and allow to dry on kitchen paper. Tip onto a baking tray and bake for 90 mins, then allow to cool (alternatively, you can use a dehydrator for this step).

Put the icing sugar in a bowl. In a large, heavy-based pan, heat the rapeseed oil to 250°C. Fry the spelt, one tbsp at a time, until it pops, puffs up and stops fizzling - around 20-30 secs. Remove the spelt, shake off any excess oil, and toss in the icing sugar. Repeat this process until all the spelt is cooked. Mix the spelt in the icing sugar thoroughly, then place in a sieve and shake off any excess sugar. The sugar puffs will keep in an airtight container for 3-4 days.

Make milk ice cream by putting 1 litre of the full-fat milk in a pan with the semi-skimmed milk, condensed milk, remaining 1 tbsp glucose and a pinch of salt. Bring to a simmer, stirring constantly. Allow to cool, churn in an ice-cream maker, then freeze.

To make the granola, heat oven to 170°C. In a frying pan, toast the puffed rice and oats for 10 mins until crisp and slightly coloured, then tip into a mixing bowl. Bring the honey, glucose and butter to the boil with a pinch of salt and cook to a light-brown caramel. Pour into the mixing bowl, stirring thoroughly until the rice and oats are coated with the caramel. Tip onto a baking tray lined with parchment paper and bake for 9 mins. Allow to cool, then store in airtight container.

To serve, place a panna cotta in the centre of a serving bowl and top with equal quantities of the sugar puffs, milk foam, granola and a scoop of ice cream.

Cin Cin

A converted garage in a North Laine backstreet is the unlikely setting for what has quickly become one of Brighton's favourite haunts for casual Italian dining. Equally unexpected is that Cin Cin's owner, David Toscano (pictured far right), was working as a lawyer in London until 12 months before opening the 18-seat counter that serves food inspired by his Calabrian heritage.

"I got to a point in my career where I just couldn't do it for another twenty-odd years. I wanted to do something that I was interested in and really cared about. I decided I wanted to open my own restaurant but I'd never even worked in one, I didn't have any experience at all," says Sydney-born Toscano, who grew up making pasta, tomato sauce and even wine with his parents and grandparents who moved from Italy to Australia in the 1950s.

Inspired by the British street-food boom and success of people like Pitt Cue Co, Toscano purchased a vintage Fiat van from a pub owner in Leeds, despite having no firm idea of what to do with it. "A friend suggested serving antipasti and prosecco - the sort of thing people love when they go to parties or a friend's house - and it just went from there."

Cin Cin debuted at Brighton's Street Diner street-food market and the Brighton Fringe Festival. David worked long hours - during evenings and while on leave from his day job – his focus never wavering from the ultimate goal of opening a restaurant. The stars aligned at a pop-up at Velo café in 2013 where Toscano first worked with Fabrizio Manconi (pictured near right), now general manager of Cin Cin, and freelance chef Jamie Halsall (pictured centre).

The trio kept in touch, with Toscano helping Halsall launch his own Brewery Kitchen pop-up, which paired craft beer with food. They considered various sites around Brighton including Sam's in Kemptown, but Vine Street became available in July 2016 and Cin Cin opened its doors in October the same year.

"What we do at Cin Cin comes very naturally to me. I don't feel like we're following any rules. Fabrizio and I have lots of memories of the food we grew up with. We can talk about those dishes in terms of stories with Jamie, and he has the technical background and skills to turn that dish into something that diners will understand and enjoy."

Cin Cin

Rabbit crochette with fresh pesto

(Serves 4)

This is a firm favourite amongst diners at Cin Cin and has been on the menu since day one. To 'pané' simply means to 'breadcrumb'.

6 rabbit legs
2 onions, roughly chopped
2 celery sticks, roughly chopped
1 leek, roughly chopped
1 garlic bulb
1 litre chicken stock
250g unsalted butter
150g flour
200g Parmesan, grated
100ml full-fat milk

For the Pesto

1 bunch basil
100g Parmesan, grated
100g pine nuts, toasted
300ml good olive oil (not extra virgin)
juice ½ lemon

For the pané

3 eggs
100ml milk
150g flour
300g dried breadcrumbs
3 litres vegetable oil (or enough to fill a deep-fat fryer or ¾ fill a large pan)

Put the rabbit legs in a large pan and add the onions, celery, leeks, whole garlic bulb and chicken stock. Bring to the simmer and cook for approximately 2 hrs or until the legs are tender and falling off the bone. Allow the rabbit to cool in the stock, then remove. Strain the stock through a sieve into a clean pan and reduce by two-thirds over a medium-high heat. Meanwhile, carefully pick the meat from the bones into a bowl, taking extra care not to leave any small bones behind.

Make a velouté sauce by melting the butter in a pan then stirring in the flour. Cook over a gentle heat for 5 mins, then gradually add the reduced stock a little at a time, whisking thoroughly to avoid lu mps. Add the Parmesan and enough of the milk to make a thick, creamy sauce. Mix well with the rabbit meat and adjust the seasoning. Allow to cool slightly.

While the rabbit is cooling, make the pesto by blending the basil, Parmesan and pine nuts together. Blend in the oil a little at a time until you have a good thick consistency without too much excess oil. Add the lemon juice to taste and adjust the seasoning.

Spoon ¼ of the cooked meat onto a sheet of cling film and roll into a neat cylindrical shape. Twist the ends of the cling film to make a tight cylinder or ballotine. Repeat with the rest of the meat, then freeze the four ballotines until firm and set. When firm enough to handle, remove the meat from the cling film and cut into equal sized rounds. Return to the freezer to firm up again.

To pané the crochette, whisk the eggs and milk together. Set out three containers, one with flour, one with the egg mixture and one with the breadcrumbs. Roll the rabbit rounds first in the flour, then the egg mixture and finally in the breadcrumbs, making sure they are evenly coated at each stage. Refrigerate until needed. The crochette can be frozen at this point but allow them to defrost fully before cooking.

To serve, heat the oil in a deep-fat fryer to 170°C and fry the crochetti for 6-10 mins. The coating should be golden brown and the inside piping hot. Serve with a spoonful of the pesto.

Slow baked celeriac with black truffle and Castelfranco

(Serves 4)

The idea for this recipe came from Cin Cin being challenged to make a 'meatier' vegetarian dish. Here, the celeriac is treated like a piece of braising meat, slow-cooked on the BBQ for several hours, transforming the flesh into something rather wonderful. Castelfranco is a mild radicchio with red-speckled, yellowish leaves that's available in winter, but butterhead lettuce makes a fine substitute.

2 large celeriac
1 tbsp olive oil
300ml milk
300ml double cream
200g block Parmesan
juice 2 lemons
1 small fresh black truffle or a jar of minced truffle salsa
2 Castelfranco or butterhead lettuces
1 small bunch chives, chopped
1-3 tbsp good olive oil

Light a BBQ or heat oven to 150°C. Put one unpeeled celeriac on a baking tray and place on the BBQ over an indirect heat or into the oven. Cook for 2½-3 hrs, turning every half hour. You'll notice it start to shrink and dehydrate. The celeriac is cooked when you can pierce it with a knife and feel no resistance, and it should be approximately two-thirds of its original size. Cover tightly to trap excess steam and allow to cool.

To make the celeriac purée, peel the remaining celeriac and cut into 2 x 2cm dice. Put in a pan with the oil and some salt and sweat slowly without colouring for 20 mins. Add the milk and cream and simmer for 20 mins more or until the celeriac is cooked through. Blend until smooth, grate in the Parmesan to taste (you won't need all of the cheese) and adjust the seasoning.

Carefully peel the skin from the cooked, cooled celeriac and tear the flesh into chunks. Put in a mixing bowl and season with salt, some of the lemon juice and the truffle.

Wash and prepare the lettuce, mix with the chives, a little lemon juice, salt and enough of the olive oil to coat. Put a large spoon of the purée into the centre of four serving plates. Lay the celeriac flesh around the purée and build the salad on top of the purée. Serve immediately.

Salad of pickled sardines, blood orange and puntarella

(serves 4)

125g salt or enough to cover the fish
8 sardines, butterflied
100ml white balsamic or similar sweet white
vinegar
juice 1 lemon
100ml good olive oil, not too peppery
2 blood oranges
1 puntarella
1 garlic clove, lightly crushed
2 rosemary sprigs

Sprinkle some of the salt liberally and evenly over a baking tray. Put the sardines, skin-side down, on the tray ensuring they don't overlap. Sprinkle the flesh side of the sardines with more salt - be liberal as it gets washed off later. Cover with cling film and refrigerate for 20 mins. Rinse the sardines under cold running water individually, rubbing all the salt off. Drain and pat dry with kitchen paper.

In a bowl, mix together the vinegar and lemon juice. In a high sided, narrow container, layer up the sardines, skin-side down, splashing some of the vinegar mix and oil over each layer. The liquid should just about cover the fish; if not, cover with cling film and lightly press down. Allow the sardines to pickle for a minimum of 2 hrs but ideally overnight.

With a sharp knife, peel the skin and pith from the blood oranges. Cut the flesh into 1cm dice, retaining any juice in a bowl. Put the segments into the bowl with the juice and reserve.

Cut the puntarella or bitter leaf into manageable pieces. Put on a baking sheet and blacken the edges with a blowtorch, taking care not to wilt the leaves too much. Add to the blood orange with the garlic and rosemary, then cover and refrigerate.

To serve, cut the sardines in half lengthways. Taste the salad and adjust the seasoning if needed. Discard the garlic and rosemary, then layer up the fish and salad on four plates, serving two sardines per portion. Finish by spooning over some of the dressing.

Sardines are a highly under-rated and under-used oily fish, packed with omega-3. The small bones are a bit tricky, so get your fishmonger to butterfly them for you. Puntarella is available from good vegetable merchants but you can substitute any bitter leaf from the chicory family.

Linguini with mussels and nduja

(Serves 4)

This is a simple but very delicious dish. Making your own fresh pasta makes all the difference here. Ask your fishmonger for the largest mussels they can find, ideally from the West Country.

700g semolina
5 whole eggs, plus 3 yolks
1 tsp olive oil, plus extra for frying
1 tsp salt
1kg mussels
1 large onion, finely diced
3 garlic cloves, finely diced
250ml white wine
400g tin good-quality chopped tomatoes
75g nduja

To make the pasta, put the semolina into a large bowl. Make a well in the centre and pour in the eggs, yolks and olive oil. Add the salt and start to slowly incorporate the eggs into the semolina with two fingers of one hand, before using both hands to really work the dough together. Turn out onto a work surface and knead to make a smooth, consistent dough. Wrap with cling film and leave for at least 2 hrs to rest.

Run the mussels under cold water for 10 mins, then go through them one by one removing any beards and making sure they are still alive and fresh. Discard any that are open or damaged.

To make the tomato sauce, sweat the onion and garlic in olive oil for 15 mins or until soft and translucent, then add 125ml white wine and reduce by half. Add the tomatoes and cook for 15 mins more.
To make the linguini, roll out the dough into a large rectangle no wider than your pasta machine. Roll the pasta through the machine on the widest setting, then roll again on the next setting down and repeat until you have worked through to the finest setting. As the dough gets thinner, its elasticity builds making for a smoother, silkier finished product.

Fold the dough back on itself so the sheet is double thickness. Adjust the setting back one notch thicker and roll the dough through again. Repeat this process at least 4 or 5 times, increasing the width setting as you go. This process is called laminating and helps to create a uniform structure to the dough. Now, proceed to work back down the thickness settings until you get to the second thinnest. You should now have an even, smooth sheet of dough.

Roll the dough through the linguini attachment of your pasta machine, if you have one, or place the sheet over a chopping board and cut evenly into thin strips. If cutting by hand, don't worry if you end up with something that looks more like tagliatelle - it won't make any difference to the finished dish and will be just as satisfying to eat.

In a large bowl, mix the mussels with the tomato sauce and the remaining 125ml wine. Bring a large pan of water to the boil. Put a heavy casserole pot on a low heat, add some olive oil and gently melt the nduja. Turn the heat back up and, just before the point of burning the nduja, pour in the mussels. Cover immediately and steam for no more than 1 min, shaking the pot constantly. Remove from the heat.

Moving quickly, put the pasta into the salted boiling water and cook for no more than 30 secs (fresh pasta cooks almost instantly in boiling water), drain and add immediately to the mussels. Stir, pour into a large sharing dish and bring to the table.

Fazzoletti with wild garlic pesto, sheep's milk ricotta and toasted almonds

(Serves 4)

Fazzoletti is a triangular shaped pasta with crinkled edges that's very easy to make. It's served here with a wild garlic pesto and sheep's milk ricotta. If you're unable to get sheep ricotta, then the cow's milk variety will do perfectly.

700g semolina
5 whole eggs, plus 3 yolks
1 tsp olive oil
1 tsp salt
250g ricotta

For the pesto

1 bunch basil
1 large handful wild garlic, leaves washed and dried, flowers reserved
100g grated Parmesan, plus extra to serve
100g toasted flaked almonds
300ml good olive oil (not extra virgin)
juice ½ lemon

Make the pasta as per the instructions in the linguini recipe on page 88. Using a pizza cutter, cut the pasta into triangle shapes approximately 5 x 5cm. Set aside while you make the pesto.

Blend together the basil, wild garlic leaves, Parmesan and almonds (reserving some almonds to sprinkle over the finished dish). Blend in the oil a little at a time until you have a good thick consistency without too much excess oil. Add the lemon juice to taste and adjust the seasoning.

Cook the pasta in salted boiling water, drain and add the pesto, spoon by spoon until the pasta is evenly coated. Grate over a little more Parmesan, spoon into four serving bowls and divide the ricotta over the top. Finish with wild garlic flowers (or baby basil leaves) and the reserved almonds.

Since opening in the Lanes in 2011, Plateau has been acclaimed as one of Brighton's best venues for food, cocktails and wine. The Guardian's wine columnist Fiona Beckett described it as 'a great natural wine bar', referring to Plateau's policy of serving natural, organic and biodynamic bottles, while the Harden's Restaurant Guide called the food 'delicious'.

Owners Thierry Pluquet (pictured far right) and Vincent Lebon (pictured right) met at university in their native France and moved to London in 2001. Both from catering families, they managed well-regarded French restaurants Le Bouchon Bordelais in Battersea and Gastro in Clapham, then moved to Brighton to manage The Saint and Blanch House in Kemptown before opening their first restaurant, Mange Tout, in 2009.

Two years later, with a successful first business under their belts and a growing interest in natural wines, Pluquet and Lebon opened Plateau, Brighton's first natural wine bar. Set over two floors with a ground-floor bar and first-floor restaurant (food is served throughout), Plateau has a Gallic feel with stained-glass windows, exposed brick, a tiled bar and lots of wood. Step inside and you're transported to a back street in Paris.

"Plateau is focused on simple dishes pinned to the authenticity of the seasonal raw ingredient, that can be shared amongst a whole table," says Pluquet. "Our desire for authenticity extends to the natural wine list. Wines with nothing added and nothing taken away, both in farming and vinification, are better for the earth, better for us and provide the truest expression of the fruit and land on which it is grown."

Chef Dan Cropper heads up the kitchen, serving a regularly changing menu of gutsy, flavour-packed dishes including the sharing meat or fish 'plateaux' that give the restaurant its name. There are plenty of French options like Rabbit crépinette with Ventreche bacon and lentils, but you'll also find the likes of tandoori mackerel with apple and beetroot or ricotta gnudi, reflecting Cropper's eclectic approach to cooking.

No visit to Plateau is complete without an expertly-made classic cocktail, made with only the best produce including freshly-squeezed citrus juices, small-batch liqueurs, vermouths and spirits from around the globe. Who could (or would want to?) resist an Ampersand made with Cognac, gin, Amaro liqueur, triple sec and bitters?

Plateau

Ham hock pakoras, masoor dal, yoghurt

(Serves 4)

A warming, comforting dish redolent with spices, this makes a perfect supper by itself or can be served as a starter. The dal is a fine accompaniment to any Indian meal.

3 ham hocks
2 carrots
6 shallots
1 thyme sprig
15 garlic cloves
1 tbsp coriander seeds
75g ginger, peeled and grated
1 tsp chilli powder
2 tbsp garam masala
7 tsp turmeric
2½ tsp ajwain seeds
250g gram flour
3 tsp asafoetida
½ tsp baking powder
2 green chillies
1 tbsp ghee or butter
200g red lentils, washed
200g yellow lentils, washed
4 tomatoes
1 tsp cumin seeds
1 tsp black mustard seeds
2tsp ground coriander
3 litres vegetable oil (or enough to fill a deep-fat fryer or ¾ fill a large pan)
natural yoghurt, to serve
coriander oil (100ml oil warmed with 1 bunch coriander), to serve.

Wash the ham hocks under cold running water, then cover with fresh water and bring to boil for a couple of mins. Drain the hocks, then put into yet more fresh water with the carrots, 2 of the shallots, thyme, 4 of the garlic cloves and the coriander seeds. Bring to the boil, then gently simmer for 4 hrs, skimming regularly, until tender and falling off the bone. Remove the hocks, retaining the stock.

Remove the fat, sinews and bones from cooled hocks. Blend 5 of the garlic cloves with 25g of the ginger, the chilli powder, garam masala, 6 tsp turmeric and 1 tsp salt, then mix with the ham hock meat. Roll the spiced meat in a double layer of cling film, twisting the ends to create a tight cylinder. Refrigerate overnight.

In a bowl, combine ½ tsp of the ajwain seeds with the gram flour, 1 tsp asafoetida and the baking powder with a pinch of salt and enough water to form a thick pakora batter.

Make masoor dal by roughly chopping the green chillies, remaining shallots and garlic cloves. Add to a pan with the remaining ginger and the ghee. Add the lentils to the pan along with the tomatoes and 1 litre strained ham hock stock. Simmer for 20-30 mins. Temper the cumin, mustard seeds, coriander and remaining turmeric in a pan over a medium heat. Add to the lentil mix, then blend until smooth before pushing through a fine strainer.

Heat the oil in a deep-fat fryer to 180°C. Cut the rolled ham hock into 30g portions. Coat in the pakora batter and deep-fry for 5 mins or until golden brown. Season well and serve in small bowls with the warmed dal, yoghurt and coriander oil.

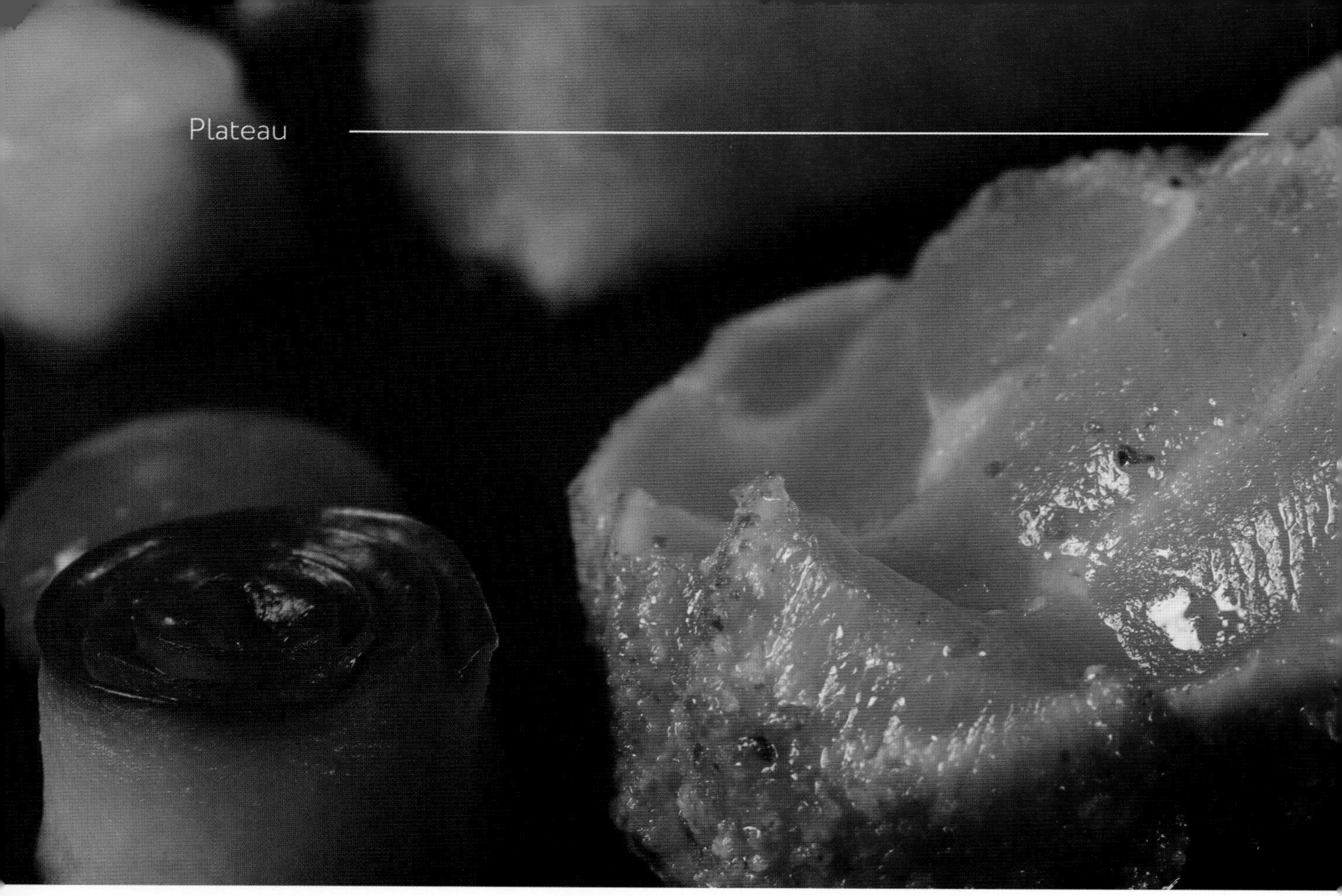

Raw salmon, watermelon, cucumber, dashi

(Serves 8)

This light and refreshing Asian-inspired dish makes a perfect starter for a dinner party as all the preparation can be done in advance. Shichimi togarashi (Japanese seven spice powder) is a useful addition to your storecupboard and is available in supermarkets.

1 side Loch Duart salmon
50g shichimi togarashi
1 watermelon

For the dashi jelly

330ml water
5g kombu
3g agar agar
15g bonito flakes

For the pickled cucumber

1 cucumber
300ml white wine vinegar
300ml white wine
150g sugar
1 tsp star anise
1 tsp coriander seeds
1 tsp cardamom seeds

Remove the belly and top end of the salmon fillet. Remove the pin bones running down the centre of the fillet with tweezers, then cut into 2 equal strips. Remove the skin and any dark-coloured flesh underneath. Cut each fillet horizontally into 4 equal pieces. Roll tightly in a double layer of cling film and regrigerate overnight.

Remove the cling film and roll the fish in the togarashi. Gently sear in a hot pan, just enough to toast the spices. Refrigerate to stop the fish cooking any further, then roll in cling film again to re-set the shape.

Cut the watermelon into finger-size rectangles, removing any skin. Blend the watermelon trimmings and push through a fine mesh sieve. Soak the watermelon rectangles in the sieved juice for 3 hrs.

To make the jelly, put the water, kombu and agar agar in a pan and simmer gently so that the temperature comes up to 62°C over a one-hour period. Add the bonito flakes and bring to the boil. Strain, refrigerate until set, then blitz to create a smooth gel.

Thinly slice the cucumber on a mandolin. Bring the vinegar, wine, sugar, star anise, coriander and cardamom to the boil in a pan. Allow to cool, then refrigerate. Put the sliced cucumber in the chilled liquor and pickle for 1 hr. Strain.

To serve, cut the salmon into 1cm thick slices, season with salt and arrange on small plates with some of the watermelon, jelly and cucumber.

Ox Cheek, turnip, Paris browns

(Serves 4)

Ox cheeks are a great-value cut and now sold in some supermarkets. They are also wonderful simply served with some mash and a green vegetable. A slow cooker is useful for this dish, or you can cut the cooking time in half by using a pressure cooker.

4 ox cheeks, trimmed of excess fat
500ml red wine
2 carrots, roughly chopped
4 shallots, roughly chopped
2 garlic cloves
1 thyme sprig
1 rosemary sprig
1 tbsp vegetable oil
1 litre veal stock or water

For the turnip dauphinoise

500ml double cream
50g fresh horseradish
8 garlic cloves
1 bunch thyme, leaves only
200g turnips
200g potatoes
100g Parmesan

For the pickled baby turnips

300ml white wine
300ml white wine vinegar
150ml sugar
1g saffron
1 tsp star anise
5 baby turnips, thinly sliced

For the mushroom tart

100g dried mushrooms
25g butter
4 shallots, sliced
4 garlic cloves
3 tbsp thyme leaves plus 1 sprig
20 Paris Brown mushrooms, plus two more thinly sliced to serve
50ml white wine
50ml double cream
250g puff pastry sheet

Marinate the ox cheeks in the wine, carrots, shallots, garlic, thyme and rosemary for 24 hrs. Remove the cheeks and vegetables, retaining the marinade. Heat oven to 140°C. Working in small batches, sear the meat and vegetables in the oil in a very hot pan until very well browned. In a separate pan, bring the retained marinade to the boil, skimming thoroughly. Strain through a clean J-cloth-lined sieve into a casserole dish. Add the veal stock or water, cheeks and vegetables and cook in the oven for 6 hrs.

Remove the cheeks from the cooking liquid, cool slightly then wrap individually in cling film and allow to set in the fridge. Strain the cooking liquid through a fine mesh sieve into a clean pan, then reduce by half over a high heat. Season before straining again.

To make the dauphinoise, heat oven to 160°C. Put the cream, horseradish, garlic and thyme in a pan, bring to the boil then simmer gently for 5 mins. Leave to infuse for at least 1 hr. Blend before straining through a fine-mesh sieve. Peel and slice the turnips and potatoes using a mandolin or as thinly as you can with a knife, then alternately layer in a baking dish with the Parmesan and the cream mix, seasoning every other layer (you should end up with 4-6 layers). Cover with baking paper, then tin foil and bake for 1 hr or until soft. Cool and cut into individual portions.

To make the pickled turnips, combine the wine, vinegar, sugar, saffron and star anise in a pan, bring to boil, then chill. Add the turnips and pickle overnight.

Make the mushroom tart. Put the dried mushrooms in a container, cover with boiling water and allow to steep overnight. Brown the butter in a pan over a medium heat. Add the sliced shallots, garlic and thyme and cook until golden brown. Roughly chop 10 of the fresh mushrooms and cook over high heat until caramelised. Add the wine and reduce until completely evaporated. Add the mushroom soaking liquid and reduce by 90 per cent, then pour in the cream and boil for 5 mins. Blend until smooth, then push through a fine mesh sieve. Season to taste.

Heat oven to 180°C. Put the pastry on a lined baking tray and spread the mushroom purée evenly over the pastry. Thinly slice the remaining mushrooms and arrange neatly over the purée. Sprinkle with thyme leaves and season. Cover with greaseproof paper and a heavy tray to keep the tart flat and bake for 30 mins. Cut into 10cm x 2cm rectangles.

To serve, warm the dauphinoise portions in the oven. Warm through the ox cheeks in the reduced cooking liquid in a pan over a medium heat. Arrange a single cheek on each plate with a portion of the dauphinoise and slice of tart. Garnish with some of the pickled turnips and the sliced raw mushrooms. Spoon over the cooking liquor to finish.

1 lamb saddle
5kg lamb bones
4 carrots, roughly chopped
8 shallots, roughly chopped
1 head of celery, roughly chopped
1 bunch rosemary
1 bunch thyme
5 garlic cloves
100ml red wine
1kg lamb's tongues
1 tbsp vegetable oil
2 tbsp butter
1 garlic clove
1 tbsp thyme leaves

For the sweetbreads

500g lamb sweetbreads
2 shallots
1 thyme sprig
3 garlic cloves
100g flour
2 eggs, beaten
1 pack panko breadcrumbs
3 litres of vegetable oil (or enough to fill a deep-fat fryer or ¾ fill a large pan)

For the wild garlic risotto

7 shallots, finely chopped
10 garlic cloves, finely chopped
60g butter
500g risotto rice
2 tbsp chopped thyme leaves, plus 3 sprigs
150ml white wine
1.1 litres chicken stock
100ml double cream
100g wild garlic
50g Parmesan

To serve

10 asparagus spears
juice and zest 1 lemon
1 tbsp thyme leaves
30g ricotta salata

Lamb cannon, braised tongue, sweetbreads, wild garlic risotto

(Serves 4)

This is a celebration of spring with seasonal wild garlic and asparagus making perfect partners for the lamb. This dish takes considerable preparation but the results are worth the effort. You'll need to order the tongue and sweetbreads in advance from your butcher. Ricotta salata is a saltier, aged version of ricotta that's similar to feta.

Debone the lamb saddle reserving the bones (alternatively, ask your butcher to do this for you), roll the fillets in double layered cling film and leave to set overnight. Heat oven to 180°C. To make the lamb stock, trim excess fat from the bones then roast them with 2 of the carrots, 4 of the shallots and half the celery until golden. Leaving the oven on, remove the roasting tin and cover the bones with water, add the rosemary, thyme and garlic, then simmer on the hob for 8-10 hrs, skimming as necessary.

Put the remaining vegetables into a roasting tin and roast in the hot oven until caramelised. Put in a pan, deglazing the roasting tin with the wine. Add the lamb stock and reduce by 70 per cent, then strain through a fine mesh sieve and reserve.

Simmer the tongues for 3-4 hrs in water. While still hot, peel and discard the skin and cut the tongues in half lengthways. To cook the sweetbreads, put the shallots, thyme and garlic in a pan with enough water to cover and bring to the boil. Add the sweetbreads and simmer for 4 mins. Remove, allow to cool, then peel off the membrane. Set out three trays or large plates: the first with the flour, a second with the whisked eggs and a third with the breadcrumbs. Roll the sweetbreads in each tray in turn, making sure they are well coated at each stage.

To make the risotto, fry 3 of the shallots and 2 garlic cloves in 15g butter. Add the rice and thyme leaves and fry for a few mins more. Add 100ml of the wine. Once absorbed, gradually add 1 litre of the stock until the rice is almost cooked, retaining some bite. Spread on a tray to cool.

Sweat the remaining shallots and garlic with the thyme sprigs in 15g butter. Add the remaining wine and cook until evaporated. Add the remaining chicken stock and reduce by 70 per cent. Add the cream and simmer for 5 mins. Strain through a fine mesh sieve to make a velouté. Blend the wild garlic until fine, then gradually add the velouté so that the garlic releases all its colour. Strain through a fine mesh sieve and reserve.

Blanch the asparagus in boiling, salted water for 2 mins and refresh in iced water. Cut the spears in half lengthways and marinate with the lemon juice, zest and thyme leaves.

When you're ready to serve, heat oven to 180°C. Sear the lamb cannons in an ovenproof pan in the oil, add the butter, garlic and thyme to the pan and roast for 4-5 mins.

Rest in a warm spot in the kitchen while you complete the dish. Use the same pan to warm through the marinated asparagus. In a separate pan, warm the lamb tongues in the reserved lamb sauce.

Heat oil in a deep-fat fryer to 180°C, then deep-fry the sweet-breads for 3 mins or until golden brown. Drain on kitchen paper.

Warm through the rice in the velouté and stir in the Parmesan, then spoon into large shallow bowls. Arrange the asparagus, sweetbreads and tongue around risotto, then slice and add lamb cannon. Crumble over the ricotta salata and serve

Basil panna cotta, strawberry, pistachio

(Serves 4)

This dessert looks stunning and tastes just as good, the savoury and sweet flavours flattering each other on the plate. The gellan gum setting agent required for this recipe is available online.

For the panna cotta

1 bunch basil
250ml cream
250ml milk
70g sugar
2½ gelatine leaves

For the pistachio soil

80g green pistachios
50g ground almonds
100g sugar
125g flour
75g melted butter

For the pistachio sponge

3 eggs
70g pistachio purée
70g sugar
20g flour

For the strawberry

500ml strawberry purée
50g icing sugar
4g gellan gum type F
200g strawberries, washed and halved
20g caster sugar
juice 1 lemon

Sesame and black pepper tuiles

75g icing sugar
25g flour
50g melted butter
70g black sesame seeds
5g black pepper

To make the panna cotta, blanch the basil in a pan of boiling water and refresh in iced water. Put in a cloth and wring out any excess liquid. Place in a blender. Warm the cream, milk and sugar together in a pan and add the gelatine. Gradually pour over the basil to release the chlorophyll, blending as you go. Strain through a fine mesh sieve, pour into 4 small pudding moulds and refrigerate until ready to serve.

To make the soil, heat oven to 90°C. Blend the pistachios to a fine powder. Add the almonds, sugar, flour and butter and blend to combine. Pour onto a baking tray lined with baking parchment and cook for 30 mins or until dried.

To make the sponge, whisk the eggs with the purée, sugar, flour and a pinch of salt to make a batter. Put in a cream whipper and charge with 3 gas bulbs. Rest the mix for 30 mins, then squirt a cupful of mixture into a 400ml plastic container. Microwave for 45 secs or until tripled in size.

To prepare the strawberries, whisk together the purée, icing sugar and gellan gum, then heat in a pan to 80°C (use a thermometer to check the temperature). Leave to set, then blend to create a fluid gel. Transfer to a plastic squeezy bottle. Cover the strawberry halves with sugar and lemon juice and leave to macerate for 1 hr.

Heat oven to 180°C. Make the tuiles by sifting the icing sugar into a mixing bowl and whisking with 20ml water. Stir in the flour and butter, followed by the sesame seeds and pepper. Spread onto a silicone baking mat or baking tray lined with baking parchment and bake for 10 mins.

To serve, unmould the panna cottas onto 4 serving plates. Dot the plates with the fluid gel. Tear off pieces of the sponge and arrange around the panna cotta. Add 2 tuiles per plate, spoon on some of the macerated strawberries and finish with the soil.

First and foremost, The Salt Room is about seafood. It's also about glamour, well-made cocktails and a great night out. It's also something of a statement. This is a big, bold place, the likes of which Brighton hadn't really seen before Raz Helalat (owner of The Coal Shed) screwed his courage to the sticking place and gave the city a truly contemporary seafront dining destination.

The roomy terrace offers views of Brighton's past and present in the form of the remains of the West Pier and the new i360 observation tower. On a sunny day, it's the ideal spot to share the signature Surf board of hot and cold crustacea. Inside there's a stunning interior by the acclaimed (and Brighton-based) Design LSM, fabulous cocktails concocted by winner of the Brighton's Best Barkeep award Matt Ottley and imaginative dishes by chef Dave Mothersill such as Whole sea bream with lemon, miso, fennel and radish.

"I worked at Terre a Terre for four years. It was an absolute eye opener. They used a lot of Asian ingredients like yuzu juice and mangosteen which has influenced my cooking," says Mothersill, who started his career aged just 15 at a Harrogate seafood restaurant and met Helalat when they both worked at The Ginger Pig.

As with The Coal Shed, the kitchen at The Salt Room centres on the charcoal-fired Josper Grill, imported from Spain. "We call ours Cheryl Coal," says Mothersill. "It's one of those pieces of equipment that you need to have experience with, practise on, nurture and spend time. Whole fish are amazing in there: mackerel, grey mullet, John Dory, plus more robust fish like gurnard and monkfish. It gives an amazing flavour and seared texture."

As former head chef of The Coal Shed, Mothersill also knows his way around a piece of meat. In addition to rib-eye and bone-in sirloin steaks, at The Salt Room you'll find such starters and mains as Lamb with garlic, radish and XO mayonnaise and Pork chop with black pudding, apple and cabbage.

Although The Salt Room can be an indulgent experience, the terrific value set lunch menu is a great way to give the place a spin. "Lunch menus can't be an afterthought, you still have to represent what you do," says Mothersill. "We want people to say, that was amazing, I'm going to come back for dinner."

The Salt Room

Crab scotch egg, curry mayonnaise, apple

(Serves 5)

A twist on the classic Scotch egg, here a soft-boiled quail's egg is covered in a delicate crab and crayfish mix and served with a mildly spicy curried mayonnaise. It changes a simple dish into a flavoursome, crowd-pleasing starter.

5 quail's eggs
200g cod
200g crayfish tails
200g white crab meat
75g brown crab meat
zest 1 lemon
2 tsp chopped chives
2 tsp chopped tarragon
3 eggs
25ml milk
250g panko breadcrumbs
250g plain flour mixed with 1 tsp salt
3 litres vegetable oil (or enough to fill a deep-fat fryer or ¾ fill a large pan)

For the curry mayonnaise

5g turmeric
5g curry powder
½ tsp coriander seeds
½ tsp cardamom seeds
500ml vegetable oil
5 egg yolks
30g Dijon mustard
30ml white wine vinegar
1 tsp salt

For the garnish

1 apple, thinly sliced
1 radish, thinly sliced
micro coriander

Get a bowl of iced water ready. Boil the eggs in salted water for exactly 2 mins 20 secs, then immediately transfer to iced water (to make peeling the eggs easier, add 50ml malt vinegar to the iced water). Softly tap the eggs on the worktop to break the shell and peel carefully.

Roughly chop the cod and crayfish, put in a food processor with the white and brown crab meat, lemon zest, chives and tarragon and pulse 2-3 times until the mixture starts to hold.

To assemble the Scotch eggs, flatten out a large spoonful of crab mixture into your hand, creating a well in the centre. Put a peeled egg in the well and gently press the mixture over to cover the egg in an even layer. Repeat with the remaining eggs and allow to set in the fridge.

Whisk the eggs and milk together, place in a tray, place the breadcrumbs in another tray, and the seasoned flour in another. Cover each Scotch egg in the flour, making sure it's evenly coated, coat in the egg wash, then roll in the bread-crumbs. Refrigerate until ready to serve.

To make the mayonnaise, slowly toast the turmeric, curry pow-der, coriander and cardamom seeds in a dry pan for 2 mins to release their natural oils and flavours. Put into a saucepan, pour over the oil and place on a low heat for 20 mins to infuse. Cool for 2 hrs, then strain.

Blend the egg yolks, mustard, white wine vinegar and salt in a food processor, then slowly add the curry oil until the mix starts to emulsify and thicken. Reserve a little oil to finish the dish.

To serve, heat oil in a deep-fat fryer to 180°C. Deep-fry the eggs for 3 mins, drain on kitchen paper, then slice in half. Put a medium sized dot of mayonnaise in the middle of 5 plates and arrange 2 egg halves on each plate. Garnish with slices of apple, radish and micro coriander and spoon over some of the reserved oil.

Raw monkfish, pickled onions, tiger's milk

(Serves 4)

You'll need to prepare the monkfish 24 hours before serving as it needs to be rolled and frozen. You can also prepare the tiger's milk at the same time - this Peruvian citrus-based marinade becomes stronger in flavour over time.

1 monkfish tail, skinned and filleted

For the tiger's milk

10g root ginger, grated
1 garlic clove, grated
¼ bunch coriander, chopped
½ tsp salt
juice 8 limes
1 tsp amarillo chilli paste, or to taste
1 shot Pisco

For the pickled onions

1 red onion, thinly sliced
1 red chilli, thinly diced
juice 2 limes
½ tsp salt

For the garnish

4 tsp crushed pistachios
1 spring onion, thinly sliced
micro coriander

Roll the monkfish fillets in cling film into a tight baton. Freeze overnight and remove 20 mins before use.

To make the tiger's milk, put the ginger, garlic, coriander and salt into a bowl, and pour over the lime juice. Add the amarillo paste (a little at a time to taste) and Pisco and whisk together. Once the ingredients have combined, let the mixture marinate for a minimum of 2 hrs, ideally overnight, then strain.

Blanch the onion for 2 mins or until translucent, strain and combine in a bowl with the chilli, lime juice and salt. Allow to cool.

To serve, cut the monkfish into 7-8 thin slices per portion and place in a circle formation on the plate. Brush with the tiger's milk and season with salt. Sprinkle 1 tsp crushed pistachios over the monkfish. Arrange pickled onion around the fish and top with some of the spring onion. Place a little micro coriander on top of the dish and serve.

Gurnard, octopus and olives

(Serves 4)

Gurnard is an under-used fish, but very sustainable and really tasty.
Elements of this dish need to be prepared 24 hours in advance.

If the octopus is frozen (this is usual), defrost and wash under running water for a few mins. Heat oven to 100°C. Put the octopus in a deep baking tray with the olive oil, chilli, rosemary, thyme, zests, fish stock, white wine and salt. Cover tightly with baking paper and tin foil and cook for 8-10 hrs or until tender.

Remove the octopus from the braising liquid and allow to cool before portioning into about 100g per person.

Make the romesco by pan-roasting the peppers, tomatoes, garlic, bread and paprika in a little of the oil until the vegetables are nicely charred. Blend with almonds and vinegar, gradually adding the oil to emulsify.

To make the olive purée, drain the olives, reserving the brine. Rinse under running water, then blend with the apple purée, spinach, oil, anchovy and 50ml of the reserved brine.

Salt the gurnard and leave for 1 hr, then wash and dry on kitchen paper.

Heat 1 tbsp rapeseed oil in a frying pan and fry the gurnard skin-side down until crisp. Flip the fish, remove from the heat and let it rest in the pan. Get another pan smoking hot, add the remaining oil and char the octopus all over.

To serve, put generous spoonfuls of the romesco and olive purée onto 4 plates, place the fish on top followed by the octopus and garnish with roasted asparagus, steamed broccoli and sea herbs or other seasonal green vegetables.

2-3kg octopus
100ml olive oil
1 red chilli
1 rosemary sprig
1 thyme sprig
zest 1 lemon
zest 1 orange
2 litres fish stock
1 litre white wine
20g salt, plus more for the gurnard
4 large gurnard fillets
2 tbsp rapeseed oil

For the romesco sauce

4 red peppers, halved and deseeded
2 tomatoes, halved and deseeded
2 garlic cloves
100g stale bread
1 pinch smoked paprika
200ml olive oil
200g toasted almonds
100ml sherry vinegar

For the green olive purée

100g pitted green olives
100g apple purée
100g baby leaf spinach
50ml olive oil
1 anchovy

Surf board

(Serves 2)

A simple yet impressive dish that's been on The Salt Room menu from day one. In essence, it's some great shellfish roasted over charcoal. We use a specially imported Josper Grill but you can achieve similar results on a barbecue.

250g mussels
250g clams
4 tbsp white wine
50g butter
4 Scottish langoustines
6 prawns
4 scallops
2 crab claws
2 oysters
50ml rapeseed oil
1 lemon, halved
2 tbsp chopped parsley

Light the barbecue and make sure it's very hot - you want to get a charred aroma and flavour on the shellfish.

Place the mussels and clams in a heatproof dish with the wine and a small knob of the butter and place over the barbecue until they open.

Season the shellfish with salt and brush lightly with rapeseed oil. Place over the fire until cooked. Once cooked brush with butter, squeeze over some lemon juice and scatter over the chopped parsley

To serve, spoon the mussels and clams into a large serving dish and pile on the fire-roasted shellfish. Spoon over all the cooking juices from the mussels and clams. Garnish with sea herbs and serve with garlic mayonnaise and Pain de campagne.

Taste of the Pier

(Serves 2-4)

A spectacular sharing dessert for two, the elements of this indulgent sweet treat change regularly with the seasons but always include a flavoured candy floss and realistic edible chocolate pebbles. The whole assembly is best left to the professionals but here are a few of the elements to try out at home.

Nutella fudge

This is a great weekend bake, perfect for a present or a great addition to ice cream and cake. You can use milk, white or dark chocolate, or replace the Nutella and chocolate with the zest of 2 lemons and 100g lemon curd for a more refreshing flavour.

400ml double cream
200g butter
525g caster sugar
100g Nutella
100g dark chocolate

Heat 350ml cream (put the remaining cream back into the fridge) with the butter and sugar in a heavy based pan and stir over a medium heat until the butter had melted. Using a thermometer, bring the mix up to 120°C, stirring often to ensure it doesn't catch. Add the remaining 50ml cold cream off the heat to reduce the temperature, whisking well. Add the Nutella and break in the chocolate and keep stirring until the mixture crystallises and begins to thicken and set. Transfer to a lined tray and set in the fridge for 2 hrs. Portion into cubes with a hot knife. Can be stored in the fridge for

Doughnuts

(Makes 20)

Doughnuts take some patience but are definitely worth the effort, and they taste so much better than shop bought, especially when still warm.

500g strong white bread flour
1 pinch salt
300ml full-fat milk
50g caster sugar,
plus extra for coating
14g fresh yeast
90g butter, softened
3 litres vegetable oil
(or enough to fill
a deep-fat fryer
or ¾ fill a large pan)

Put the flour and salt in a bowl. Using a thermometer, bring the milk and sugar to 37°C in a pan, then take off the heat. Whisk to dissolve the sugar, add the yeast, then pour into the bowl with the flour. Bring together with your hands until you have a rough dough. Work the butter into the dough, then transfer to a work surface and knead for 10 mins to make the dough smooth and firm. Transfer to an oiled bowl and prove for 1 hr.

Turn out onto a lightly floured work surface and roll out to a thickness of 1 inch. Cut into rounds the size of your choice and transfer to a lined tray. Re-roll the dough once more to get a second batch. Leave the doughnuts for about 30 mins in a warm place to double in size. Heat the oil in a deep-fat fryer to 170°C. Fry the doughnuts for 3 mins, then carefully flip them over in the oil and fry for 3 mins more (the cooking time will depend on the size of the doughnuts). Drain on kitchen paper and roll in caster sugar.

You can flavour the sugar with vanilla, cinnamon or lemon zest, and fill the doughnuts with lemon curd, Nutella or custard if you like.

Peanut butter '99' ice cream

This is best made in an ice-cream machine but can be frozen in a container and stirred every hour until set – though the result won't be as smooth. Trimoline and xanthan gum are available online.

500ml milk
500ml cream
100g sugar
100g trimoline
4g xanthan gum
100g peanut butter

Place the milk and cream in a pan. Using a thermometer, bring up to 88°C and add the sugar, trimoline, xantham gum and peanut butter, whisking to dissolve all the ingredients. Using a hand blender, mix until smooth, then strain through a fine mesh sieve. Chill in the fridge, then churn in an ice-cream machine. Pop into a container and freeze until needed.

Chocolate truffles

This is a more simple version of The Salt Room's famous 'edible pebbles', which are made using white chocolate, icing sugar and black food colouring. Here, you can simply dust the balls with cocoa powder to make chocolate truffles. For a delicious twist, add orange zest, vanilla or 50ml brandy or Cointreau to the recipe.

200ml double cream
50g butter
50g glucose
300g dark chocolate, broken into pieces
cocoa powder, for dusting

Whisk together the cream, butter and glucose in a pan and bring to the boil. Take off the heat, pour over the chocolate and whisk until smooth and glossy. Allow to firm up in the fridge. When firm, use a spoon to scoop into small balls. Dust generously with cocoa powder, then refrigerate until firm and set.

To serve, depending on how many people are sharing this dessert, place a few doughnuts onto a large wooden board with some truffles and pieces of fudge alongside. Scoop the ice cream into small bowls and place on the board with small spoons.

115

Douglas McMaster (pictured right) is one of Brighton's most exciting and influential young chefs. Named by Vogue magazine as one of the '20 Names of Now' (a list of young innovators redefining their fields), McMaster has gained national attention for his sustainable and ethical approach to cooking at Silo, the restaurant he helped launch in Autumn 2014 in a Victorian warehouse in Brighton's bohemian North Laine.

The column inches about the 50-seater restaurant, café and bakery have stacked up, detailing McMaster's 'pre-industrial food system' and 'zero waste' philosophy achieved with the help of an in-house composting machine, plates made from recycled plastic bags, electrolysed oxidised water for cleaning instead of chemicals and local, sustainable and foraged produce delivered in reusable containers.

In addition to milling ancient varieties of wheat such as Einkorn and Amaretto in the restaurant for Silo's superlative 48-hour sourdough bread, McMaster makes his own butter, yoghurt and curd and has any number of ingredients fermenting in his basement kitchen, including red cabbage which he might serve with slow-cooked Jerusalem artichokes and blue cheese.

McMaster, whose impressive CV includes St John Bread and Wine in London, Noma in Copenhagen, Faviken in Sweden and Attica in Melbourne, as well as the title of BBC Young Chef of the Year, has made a roaring success of this bold venture, serving up to 400 people on a Saturday from breakfast through to dinner, and garnering rave reviews from the likes of Giles Coren of The Times, who called Silo a 'a brilliant, sexy, local, planet-conscious place'.

McMaster is evolving a culinary identity and a lexicon of foraged ingredients - including Alexanders, sea buckthorn and pine – that are all his own. They inform the restaurant's three dinner menus, entitled 'Dairy' 'Fish' and 'Meat' that allow vegetarians, pescatarians and meat eaters to enjoy Silo's unique cuisine. "The food is a reflection of my ideas, which are based on fundamental ecological principles," says McMaster. "I like the idea of organic farming systems where everything is considered in a natural cycle. I find that really inspiring and I want to represent that on a plate of food by accommodating what's abundant and available."

Silo

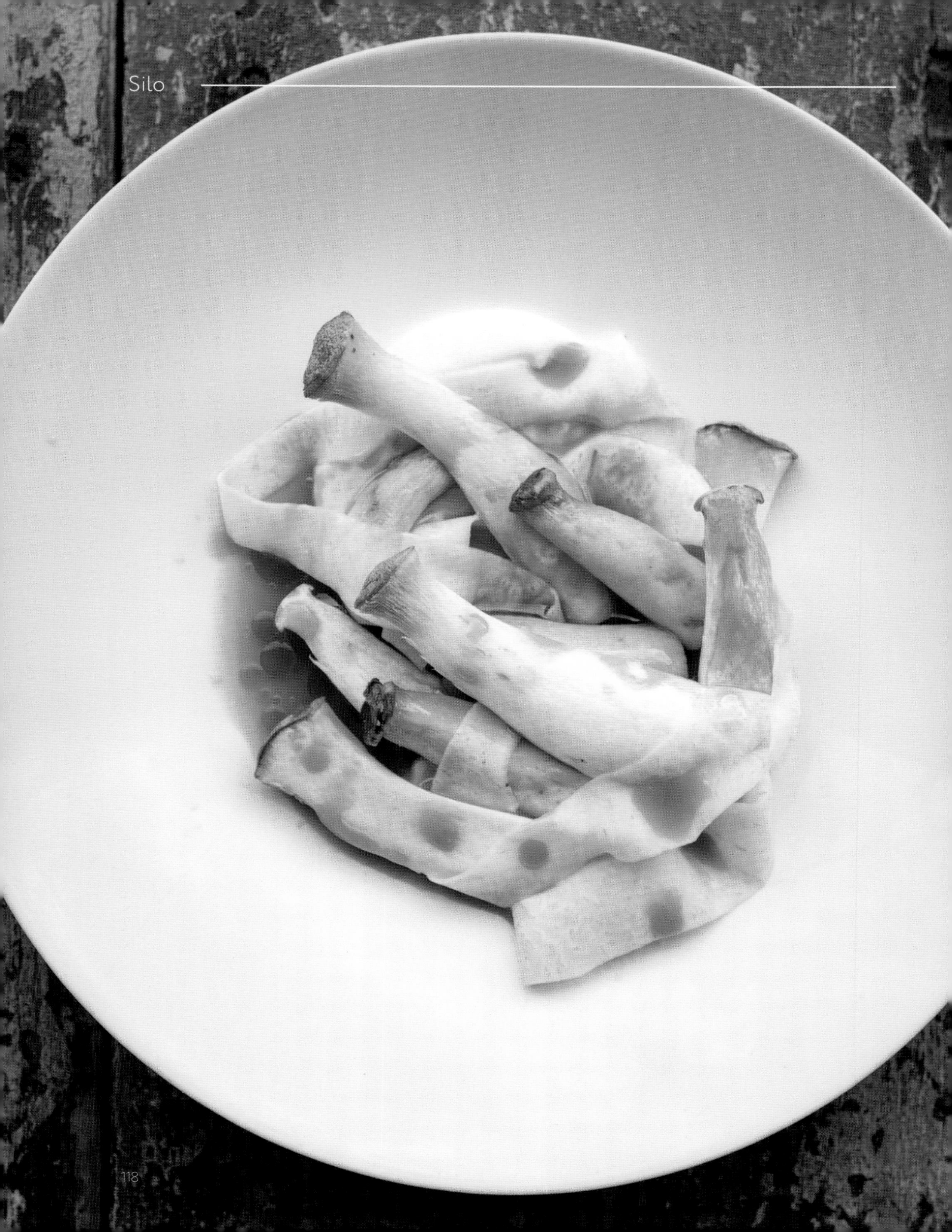

King oyster mushrooms, rosemary, celeriac

(Serves 4-6)

This dish is a real crowd pleaser as good-quality mushrooms can satisfy any carnivore, and the rich umami flavour of the broth merges harmoniously with the creamy flavours of the celeriac. You'll need to plan ahead, however, as the celeriac needs to be pickled for at least 24 hours and the mushroom broth takes several hours to cook.

At least one day in advance, peel the celeriac with a large, sharp knife. Using a mandolin or spiraliser, cut the celeriac into 1mm thick ribbons. Make a pickling liquor by whisking the vinegar and sugar together in a bowl with 150ml water until the sugar has dissolved. Place one-third of the celeriac in the solution (reserve the other two-thirds to make a purée) making sure it's completely submerged and refrigerate for at least 24 hrs.

Put the remaining celeriac scraps and butter in a heavy-based pot with a good pinch of salt and sweat over a low heat with the lid on for 20 mins or until soft, checking from time to time that the celeriac stays pale and doesn't caramelise. Blend until very smooth (if the blender struggles, add a small amount of water, however you want this purée to be as thick as possible). Allow to cool and refrigerate until needed.

Heat oven to 200°C. Sort through the mushrooms, reserving 300g of the best. Brush the remaining 500g with oil and season with salt. Roast for 4 mins or until golden brown. Transfer to a pot, cover with water and simmer for 3-4 hrs until all the flavour is released from the mushrooms. Turn up the heat and reduce the liquid until it's an intense mushroom flavour. Check the seasoning.

Make the rosemary oil by blanching the parsley in boiling water, refreshing in cold water and squeezing out the excess moisture. Blend with 25g of the rosemary and the 100ml oil, then strain through a muslin cloth.

When you are ready to serve, roast 200g of the remaining mushrooms as above, slice the final 100g into 2mm-thick slices and finely chop the remaining 10g rosemary (use a sharp knife to prevent bruising which dulls the herb's flavour). Reheat the celeriac purée over a medium heat, stirring so that it doesn't catch or colour.

Put 1 tbsp warm celeriac purée onto each plate, followed by some of the roasted mushrooms and equal quantities of raw mushroom slices and pickled celeriac. Pour 2 tbsp hot broth carefully around the peripheries of the plate followed by a good drizzle of rosemary oil and a pinch of finely chopped rosemary. Serve immediately.

1 large celeriac
100ml cider vinegar
50g sugar
150g unsalted butter
800g king oyster mushrooms
100ml rapeseed oil (not cold pressed), plus 4 tbsp for roasting
25g parsley
35g rosemary

Raw Gurnard, oyster and broccoli

(Serves 4-6)

This is a completely raw dish so make sure you've got the freshest seafood possible. The combination of raw broccoli with oyster is a winning one and the presentation is minimal, elegant and unpretentious.

1 gurnard, filleted, skinned and pin bones removed
1 small head of broccoli
3 oysters
200ml rapeseed oil
juice 1 lemon

Dice the gurnard flesh into chunky pieces (if you cut it too fine it will be like pâté) and refrigerate. With a turning knife, cut the very top tips of the broccoli into small, caviar-like pieces (save the core to use in another dish).

Shuck the oysters into a tall narrow jug, removing any broken shell. Using a hand blender, slowly add the oil and blend to an emulsified, mayonnaise-like consistency. Add some of the lemon juice to taste.

To plate the dish, season the fish with rock salt, and dress the broccoli with rock salt and the remaining lemon juice to taste. Place a 15cm ring mould in the centre of each plate and spoon in an even layer of the gurnard about a thumbnail deep. Squeeze a few generous blobs of the oyster emulsion randomly on the fish, then cover with an even layer of broccoli to completely hide the fish and emulsion. Carefully remove the mould. Serve immediately.

Braised ox cheek, patty pans, tarragon

(Serves 4-6)

At the restaurant, we use ox cheek for this recipe but it will work with any tough cut of meat. Patty pan is a unique ingredient: a beautiful flying-saucer shaped squash, its curves highlighted here by the raw slices. The choice of pot for this recipe is crucial - choose one that will allow you to cover the meat with the stock without having to top up with water.

Trim the ox cheek of any sinew and fat and cut into 4-6 pieces, or ask your butcher to do this for you.
Sweat down the onions in a heavy-based pot with 50g of the butter and a big pinch of salt over a low heat. When they start to soften, cover and continue to cook until they become very mushy. Remove the lid, turn up the heat slightly and cook until the onions caramelise and are golden in colour, stirring occasionally.

Season the ox cheek, roast in a hot frying pan with 1 tbsp oil to heavily caramelise the meat, then transfer to the pot of onions. With the heat still medium to low, add 30ml vinegar and allow to reduce. Heat oven to 120°C. Top up the pan with stock, bring to a gentle simmer, cover, then transfer to the oven and cook for 2 hrs or until you can easily push a butter knife through the meat but it remains in one piece.

Using a mandolin, cut 4-5 perfect slivers of patty pan per portion. Neatly stack them so they don't oxidise, wrap and refrigerate until needed. In a suitable sized pot with a heavy base, slowly sweat the remaining patty pan scraps in 100g butter and a good pinch of salt with the lid on until very soft (about 20 mins). Keep the heat low, making sure the squash remains pale and doesn't caramelise. Blend to a smooth purée, season and keep warm in a container with a lid on.

Blanch the parsley in boiling water, refresh and squeeze out excess moisture. Put the parsley, rosemary, 50g tarragon and 100ml oil into a blender and blend until smooth, then strain through a muslin cloth.

Strain the beef braising juice through a fine sieve. Heat 200g of the strained juice in a pan and slowly whisk in the remaining 100g butter, which should slightly thicken the sauce. Add seasoning and some of the remaining vinegar to taste.

Spoon 1 large tbsp purée into the centre of each plate, followed by a piece of ox cheek. Gently spoon 1 tbsp beef sauce over and around the plate. Evenly distribute the remaining fresh tarragon randomly on each plate. Lightly dress the slices of squash in the remaining sherry vinegar and rock salt and drape over the whole dish. Finish with a good squeeze of herb oil.

1kg ox cheek
500g white onions, sliced
250g unsalted butter
100ml rapeseed oil (not cold-pressed), plus 1 tbsp for frying
50ml sherry or cider vinegar
1 litre beef stock
4 small patty pans
50g parsley
50g rosemary
75g tarragon

Sea buckthorn, brown butter, Douglas fir

(Serves 4-6)

"This is the Silo classic, celebrating 'off grid ingredients' or the untapped abundance of nature. The dish needs precise execution to create the 'f**k me moment' of which this dish has that rare potential." Douglas McMaster

For the brown butter mousse

500ml double cream
450ml whipping cream
250g butter
1 tbsp milk powder
125g sugar
50ml honey
200g egg yolks
10g gelatine

For the granité

250ml sea buckthorn juice
250ml water
50g sugar

For the rye crumb

100g butter
100g rye flour
90g strong white flour
80g sugar
4g salt

For the Douglas fir oil

25g parsley
25g Douglas fir needles
100ml rapeseed oil (not cold pressed)

For the jelly

3 bronze gelatine leaves
250ml sea buckthorn juice
175g sugar
250ml filtered water or mineral water

Make the brown butter mixture by putting 500ml double cream, the butter and milk powder in a heavy based pan on a low heat. Whisk regularly until the mixture separates and the proteins solidify and go a golden brown. Pass through a muslin cloth, squeezing out any excess butter.

Put the sugar and honey in a small saucepan, add 1 tbsp water and bring to 120°C over a medium heat. Meanwhile, whip the egg yolks in a stand mixer until fluffy. With the mixer on medium speed, slowly pour the sugar mixture over the yolks. Once the sugar is incorporated, leave the mixer on a slow speed until the bowl cools to room temperature.

Soften the gelatine in water for 5 mins. Drain, squeezing the water from the gelatine, then melt in a pan over a low heat with 1 tbsp of the whipping cream. Cool to room temperature.

Gently whip the remaining whipping cream and gelatine cream mixture in a large bowl to soft peak stage. Fold the egg yolk mixture, whipped cream mixture and brown butter solids together using a rubber spatula as if making a soufflé (you may need to crumble in the brown butter solids by hand). Transfer to a plastic container and leave to set in the fridge.

To make the granité, combine the sea buckthorn juice with the water and sugar in a plastic container and put in the freezer. As it starts to freeze, run a fork through the mixture so that it forms granules. Repeat at regular intervals until the granité is fully frozen.

To make the rye crumb, heat oven to 160°C. Put the butter in a heavy based pan over a low heat and gently cook until it smells nutty, turns an amber colour and stops sizzling. Pour through a fine sieve into a glass or metal bowl to remove any solids. Mix with the remaining rye crumb ingredients by hand or in a stand mixer until the mixture resembles a classic crumble. Spread out on a silicone baking mat or baking parchment-lined baking tray and bake until light golden brown. Gently fold the mixture around the trays to achieve an even cooking. Allow to cool.

To make the Douglas fir oil, blanch the parsley in boiling water, refresh in iced water then squeeze out any excess moisture. Put the parsley, fir needles and oil in a blender and process until smooth, then pass through a clean muslin cloth. The oil can be made ahead and kept in the freezer.

To make the jelly, soften the gelatine in water for 5 mins, drain and squeeze out any excess water. In a small pan melt the soaked gelatine with 1 tbsp sea buckthorn juice, then combine with the remaining sea buckthorn juice, sugar and water. Transfer to the fridge until it begins to thicken (thickening the mixture before setting will prevent the final jelly from splitting). When thickened, whisk the mixture and pour into 4-6 dariole moulds.

To plate the dish, quickly dip the jelly mould into hot water then turn out onto a shallow bowl, just off-centre. Add 1 tbsp of the brown butter mousse alongside the jelly and cover with the rye crumb. Add 1 tbsp Douglas fir oil to the base of the dish and finish with 1 tbsp granité.

Yorkshire rhubarb, raw cacao, lemon thyme

(Serves 4)

The combination of these ingredients is as glorious as it is unique. About 80% of cacao is wasted in the chocolate-making process and this dish highlights how versatile the by-product of the process can be; as well as being delicious, cacao nibs have a great nutty texture. Yorkshire rhubarb is one of the best products on Earth and is ideal for the dish, alternatively field (summer) rhubarb will suffice.

600g rhubarb
150g caster sugar
juice 3 lemons
3 eggs
100ml double cream
1 small bunch lemon thyme, leaves picked, stalks reserved
150g cacao nibs and/or shells

Trim the rhubarb and cut into batons. Using a mandolin, cut the batons into 1mm-thick 'planks' and set aside. Stew the rhubarb trim with 25g sugar in a pan over a medium heat. Remember that you're not making a jam, but a nice tart rhubarb compote. Allow to cool, then refrigerate.

To make the cacao parfait, whisk the lemon juice, eggs and remaining sugar together in a large bowl until the sugar has dissolved. Bring the double cream and thyme stalks to the boil, strain over the egg mix and whisk well to combine.

Heat oven to 140°C. Choose 4 silicone moulds that can individually contain 60-100ml (the shape doesn't matter for this dessert as the parfait is hidden underneath the rhubarb). Pour 50g of the parfait mixture into each of the moulds and place 1 tsp cacao nibs or shells into each one. Carefully transfer to the oven and cook for 20-40 mins or until the parfait has set. Remove and leave to cool.

Spoon 1 tsp compote onto 4 cold plates and un-mould one of the parfaits on top of the compote. Spoon another teaspoon of compote over each parfait, then carefully arrange the raw rhubarb 'planks' over the dish, hiding the parfait and compote. Sprinkle each plate generously with lemon thyme leaves and serve immediately.

For a chef, Atlanta-born Orson Whitfield (pictured far right) was a late starter. After studying Business Administration and Finance and interning for a bank in America, he'd reached the grand age of 26 before landing his first cheffing job at Selsdon Park Hotel in Croydon. "I felt at home in the kitchen right away," says Whitfield who moved to the UK 17 years ago to study Hospitality at Thames Valley University and Westminster College. "My Mum is Italian and Italy is where I fell in love with food, but as both of my parents cooked, food was already a big part of my life."

He lived in Surrey with his wife Linda (pictured right) for more than a decade, working in and around the county, including a stint as head chef at a restaurant in Teddington before relocating to Brighton with plans to open their own place. "There weren't many sites about but I saw an opportunity to run the kitchen at The Geese pub in Hanover. It's one of the toughest things to do: all of the cooking and cleaning, everything by yourself, but it showed me that I could do quite a bit in a small space."

After a successful year running The Shakespeare's Head pub near Brighton station as a couple, the Whitfields finally found a site on Baker Street, a side street off London Road famous locally as the location of Bardsley's, one of the city's best-loved fish and chip shops.

Opened in 2014, Semolina is a quintessential family-run neighbourhood restaurant, with an intimate dining room simply decorated with antique mirrors and set with bare wood tables and bistro-style chairs. Linda runs front of house with charm (and mixes a mean cocktail) while Orson takes care of the culinary side with a modern European menu that might include dishes such as Lamb rump with skordalia and pancetta.

Everything - including two types of notably good sourdough bread, pasta and ice cream - is made from scratch using produce sourced from the Open Market (virtually next door to Semolina), HISBE ethical supermarket in London Road that stocks produce from Sussex farms, and local foragers that drop ingredients off at the door. "We're lucky to have so much on our doorstep," says Orson. "The food is quite simple and ingredient-led because this is a bistro environment, we don't try to complicate things too much."

Semolina

Sea Bream, Miso Cauliflower, Black Sesame

(Serves 4)

This dish is healthy and light, yet bursting with flavour. Sea bream has an excellent flavour and is great value, and sea bass or grey mullet would also work well.

4 sea bream fillets (140-170g each)
1 head of cauliflower
1-2 tbsp vegetable oil
2 tbsp white miso paste
1 shallot, chopped
1 garlic clove, chopped
50ml milk
75ml double cream
50ml tamari soy sauce
25ml mirin
25ml sesame oil
12 leaves pak choi
1 tbsp toasted black sesame

Trim the sea bream and check for any pin bones by gently running your finger down the centre of the fillet and removing with tweezers. Cut the cauliflower in half. Chop one half and set aside, then cut the other half into four steaks about 2 fingers thick each. Season with salt and seal in a hot pan with some of the oil. Mix the miso with a little water to form a paste and brush on to the cauliflower steaks.

Sweat the shallot and garlic on a low heat in a large pan in some of the oil until soft but not coloured. Add the chopped cauliflower along with the milk and double cream and cook until soft. Season and purée in a blender.

Mix the soy sauce, mirin and sesame oil together in bowl to make a dressing.

Heat oven to 180°C. Roast the cauliflower steaks for 5-7 mins. Pan-fry the bream fillets in a non-stick pan on medium heat skin-side down with some of the oil until crisp. Sauté the pak choi with some of the oil in a pan until tender, seasoning to taste. To serve, re-heat the cauliflower purée and spoon some into the centre of four warmed plates. Top with a miso cauliflower steak, some of the pak choi and a bream fillet. Spoon over the dressing and garnish with the black sesame.

Roasted poussin, carrot gnocchi, ginger broth

(Serves 4)

4 poussin
1 celery stick
4 carrots
1 shallot
1 medium onion
1 leek
50g fresh ginger
1 star anise
2 garlic cloves
2 medium potatoes (150g cooked weight)
2 egg yolks
75g plain flour
2 tbsp vegetable oil
1 knob of butter
1 head of kale or other leafy green vegetable, finely sliced

For the carrots

25g unsalted butter
2 medium carrots, halved lengthways
pinch salt
pinch sugar
1 tbsp water

Heat oven to 180°C. Cut the poussin into four pieces each, two legs and two breasts. Roast the remaining carcasses with the celery, 1 carrot, shallot, onion and leek (all roughly chopped) for 45 mins or until the bones are browned (check after 30 mins). Keeping the oven on, transfer the carcasses to a stock pot or large pan, add the ginger, star anise and garlic, and cover with 1 litre of cold water. Bring to a simmer for 1½ hrs. Strain, return to the heat and reduce by half over a high heat. Season to taste and set aside.

Bake the potatoes uncovered at 180°C for 1 hr or until soft. Meanwhile, slice the remaining carrots and heat in a covered pan with 1 tbsp water and a pinch of salt and sugar until soft. Purée in a blender. Scoop the flesh from the cooked potatoes into a bowl and mash. Add the carrot purée, yolks and flour and mix well to form a ball (if the mixture is sticky, add a little more flour).

Form the mixture into long cylinders, then cut into pillow-like sections with a knife. Bring a large pan of salted water to a simmer (do not allow to boil) and fill a large bowl with iced water. Poach the gnocchi a few at a time; they are ready when they rise back to the surface. Transfer to the ice bath immediately to stop cooking. Drain on kitchen paper and reserve.

Oil the poussin pieces, season with salt and seal in a smoking pan until brown on all sides. Transfer the legs only to the oven and roast at 180°C for 12 mins, adding the breasts for the final 5 mins of cooking. The poussin is ready when juices run clear at the leg joints. Allow to rest for a few mins while you cook the gnocchi in a non-stick pan with the butter (the kale or other greens can be heated in the same pan). Re-heat the broth.

Melt the butter in a frying pan and add the carrots flat-side down, keeping the heat low to medium. Add the salt, sugar, water and cover. The carrots are ready when a skewer pierces through the thick end with a little resistance.

Place a mound of the kale or greens in the centre of each of four plates and arrange two legs and two breasts on top. Cut each carrot in half again at an angle and place two pieces on each plate. Arrange some of the gnocchi on each plate and pour the ginger stock around. Serve immediately.

A dish for in-between seasons when winter is not done but spring has not sprung. Use floury potatoes such as Maris Piper or King Edward to make the gnocchi.

Lentil, swede and Medita samosas, rhubarb chutney

(Serves 4)

Chef Orson learned to make samosa pastry from an Indian chef living in Thailand and has adapted the recipe to incorporate Sussex produce in the form of Medita cheese from High Weald Dairy. You can substitute any good-quality barrel-aged feta cheese.

2 cardamom pods, seeds only
½ tsp cumin seeds
½ tsp coriander seeds
1 shallot, diced
5cm piece ginger, chopped
1 garlic clove
30g swede, diced
30g puy lentils, cooked
squeeze lime juice
65g Medita or feta cheese
125g plain flour
125g gram flour
½ tsp ground fenugreek
5g salt
50ml rapeseed oil
3 litres vegetable oil (or enough to fill a deep fat fryer or ¾ fill a large pan)

For the rhubarb chutney

200g rhubarb, roughly chopped
75g sugar
50ml red wine vinegar
5cm piece ginger
2 cardamom pods

For the salad

1 small handful coriander, leaves torn
8 mint leaves, leaves torn
4 radishes, thinly slices
1 tbsp diced swede, boiled until tender
1 tbsp rapeseed oil

Toast the cardamom, cumin and coriander seeds and grind in a spice grinder. Sweat the shallots with the ginger and garlic, add the ground seeds, swede and 2 tbsp water. Season and cook until the swede is soft. Add the cooked lentils, lime and crumble in the cheese. Refrigerate.

Mix together the flours, fenugreek, salt and rapeseed oil with 70ml water until the ingredients form a ball. Knead for 5 mins, wrap in cling film and refrigerate for 30 mins.

Make the chutney by putting all the ingredients in a pan over a low heat and stirring occasionally until nearly all liquid has reduced. Allow to cool.

Heat the oil in a deep-fat fryer to 170°C. Roll out the pastry very thinly and cut into discs the size of the top of a pint glass. Brush with water, place 2 tsp of the filling in the centre of each disc and fold the pastry over the filling to form a triangle, making sure the parcel is sealed. Place on oiled greaseproof paper to avoid sticking. Deep-fry in hot oil until golden, then drain on kitchen paper.

Make the salad by combining the coriander, mint and radish with the diced swede. Toss with rapeseed oil and season to taste. Serve two samosas per person with some of the chutney and salad.

Semolina

Peanut butter cheesecake, dark chocolate sorbet

(Serves 4)

This delicious dessert brings back childhood memories for Orson who grew up in America where peanut butter is king. It will always be a winning combination with chocolate.

Put the gelatine leaves in cold water to soften. In a stand mixer, beat the egg yolks with the sugar and flour until pale and fluffy. Heat the milk with the vanilla pod to just under boiling point. Slowly pour half the milk onto the egg mixture, then return to the pan with the remaining milk and stir over a low heat for 5-10 mins until thickened (this is called pastry cream). Remove from the heat, cover with cling film and allow to cool slightly.

Blitz the digestives in a food processor and stir in the melted butter. Use the mix to line the bottom of four 7cm x 3.5cm ring moulds or a 20cm cake tin to form the base of the cheesecake and refrigerate.

Once the pastry cream is just warm to the touch, squeeze the excess liquid from the gelatine and fold into the pastry cream until completely dissolved. Push through a sieve and stir in the cream cheese, peanut butter and icing sugar. Fill the moulds or cake tin with the mixture, smoothing over the top with a palette knife and refrigerate for 3-4 hrs.

Make the sorbet by heating the water, chocolate, cocoa powder, caster sugar, glucose and salt together. Stir until all the ingredients have dissolved into the water. Pass through a sieve into a container set over an ice bath to cool. Refrigerate for a few hrs then churn in an ice cream maker.

Half an hour before the cheesecakes are set, make the chocolate glaze by dissolving the gelatine in some cold water. Heat the caster sugar and cocoa powder in 100ml water until dissolved and allow to cool slightly. Squeeze out the excess liquid from the gelatine, add to the cocoa mixture and whisk thoroughly. Spoon over the cheesecakes and return to the fridge for an hour.

To make the fudge, heat the peanut butter, butter and salt until the butter has melted. Sift the icing sugar over the mixture and fold until smooth. Transfer to a tray and chill until set hard. Dice before serving.
Serve an individual cheesecake or slice from a large cake with a scoop of the sorbet and some of the peanut butter fudge.

1.5 leaves gelatine
3 large egg yolks
65g caster sugar
40g plain flour
250ml full-fat milk
1 vanilla pod
100g digestive biscuits
50g butter, melted
300g full-fat cream cheese at room temperature
175g smooth peanut butter
60g icing sugar, sifted

For the chocolate sorbet

500ml water
100g dark chocolate (min 64% cocoa solids)
100g Dutch cocoa powder
75g caster sugar
100ml liquid glucose
pinch of salt

For the chocolate glaze

1 leaf gelatine
25g caster sugar
15g Dutch cocoa powder
100ml water

For the peanut butter fudge

125g smooth peanut butter
90g unsalted butter
1 pinch salt
185g icing sugar

Rhubarb curd meringue tart, buttermilk ice cream

(Serves 4)

This is a great tart to welcome in the spring and, coupled with the buttermilk ice cream, it's a sign of lighter things to come. Make the ice-cream base a day ahead, then churn on the day you want to serve the tart.

For the buttermilk ice cream

300ml buttermilk
150ml double cream
100ml milk
100ml glucose
50ml vodka or gin
2 medium eggs
75g caster sugar

For the tart

7 eggs
175g butter
65g icing sugar
125g plain flour
350g rhubarb
280g caster sugar
½ tsp ground ginger
40ml water
30g liquid glucose

For the rhubarb and mint garnish

1 rhubarb stalk
100ml water
100g sugar
small leaf tops from a bunch of mint

To make the ice cream, put the buttermilk, double cream, milk, glucose and vodka or gin in a pan and heat to just under boiling point. Whisk the eggs and sugar together until pale, then pour the buttermilk mixture over while still whisking. Return the mix to the pan and, stirring constantly to avoid curdling, heat to 84°C or until the mixture coats the back of a wooden spoon. Pour into a container set over iced water and chill for 1 hr. Refrigerate for 6-8 hrs or overnight.

Now make the tart. Separate the eggs, placing 6 yolks together in one bowl and 1 yolk in a separate bowl. Put 3 of the whites in another bowl, keeping the remaining 4 for another dish. Mix the single yolk with 50g of the butter and the icing sugar, then gradually add the flour and mix gently until it forms a ball of pastry. Refrigerate for 1 hr.

Roll the pastry to a thickness of a pound coin. Line a 27.5cm tart tin or 4 individual 10cm tartlet tins and refrigerate again for 30 mins. Heat oven to 200°C. Line the pastry with greaseproof paper, fill with baking beans and blind-bake for 10 mins. Remove the greaseproof paper and beans, lower oven to 180°C and bake the pastry for 5 mins. Allow to cool on a rack.

Turn the oven down to 120°C. Make the tart filling by heating the rhubarb with 100g of the caster sugar in a pan over a medium heat until soft, then purée in a blender until smooth. Put the purée in a bowl set over hot water, add the remaining butter and stir until melted. Add the remaining yolks and stir constantly for 10-15 mins or until the mixture is thickened, then stir in the ginger. Fill the tart case or tartlet cases with the mixture and bake for 15 mins or until set.

Make Italian meringue by heating the water, remaining caster sugar and glucose in a pan to 120°C (use a sugar thermometer to check the temperature). Using the whisk attachment of a stand mixer, beat the 3 egg whites to soft peaks. With the mixer running, pour the sugar mixture slowly over the whites, then continue to whisk at medium speed for 10 mins to stiff peaks. Transfer to a piping bag and pipe generously over the tart or tartlets. Torch lightly with a blowtorch for a charred effect.

To make the garnish, peel the rhubarb into strips and cut into 2.5cm batons. Make a simple syrup by heating together the water and sugar until the sugar has dissolved, then simmer on a low heat for 10 mins. Allow to cool slightly, then pour over the rhubarb and leave to cool. This should partially cook the rhubarb and retain a bite.

To serve, churn the ice cream in an ice-cream maker. Serve a slice of tart or individual tartlet with a scoop of the ice cream decorated with alternating strips of rhubarb and mint leaves.

The Gingerman

Brighton-born Ben McKellar is the godfather of the city's restaurant scene. Former employees of his four-strong Gingerman Restaurants Group (no surprise that McKellar is a redhead), which includes The Ginger Pig in Hove, The Ginger Dog in Kemptown and The Ginger Fox in the South Downs, have gone on to run and work at some of the city's most notable establishments: Raz Helalat (former restaurant manager of the Ginger Pig, now owner of The Coal Shed and The Salt Room); Dan Kenny (former head chef of The Gingerman, now chef at The Set and Dizzy Gull) and Dave Mothersill (former head chef at The Ginger Pig, now head chef at The Salt Room).

"There are lots of guys around town who've worked for us. There's a real cooking community which I think is great," says McKellar, who opened The Gingerman in 1998 when he was just 24 with his wife Pamela, 21 at the time. McKellar packed a lot into a few short years before becoming his own boss, with time spent working in Provence, two Michelin-starred L'Ortolan outside Reading and a deluxe bistro on Park Avenue in New York.

"I learnt more in the year I was in New York than I did anywhere else in terms of what I do now, which is accessible, tasty, well-produced food," says McKellar, who was inspired to open The Gingerman in a 'bank-rupt backstreet Irish pub' by his former head chef, the late and well-respected Mark Emmerson who ran One Paston Place in Kemptown in the 90s.

Early menus included the likes of rack of lamb and duck breast, de rigueur at the time, but have constantly evolved. McKellar now oversees all four kitchens in the group but works closely with Gingerman head chef Mark Charker (pictured far right) on dishes such as Monkfish with Parma ham and red pepper and chorizo arancini. "Mark was sous chef at The Ginger Fox and has also worked at Ockenden Manor. I've always really liked his food and now he's really running with it."

The Gingerman will celebrate two decades in business in 2018, but McKellar isn't standing still. "I'm always look-ing at sites and we've got a few ideas that will be slightly different from what we already do, but it's got to be right. We're not looking for Michelin stars, just for people to be happy."

The Gingerman

Ridgeview Estate Spa...
Bloomsbury Btl £45 Gls
Fitzrovia Btl £49.50 G...
Blanc de Blancs Btl £...

Cured and smoked Sussex coast mackerel, cucumber, wasabi

(Serves 4)

Mackerel is a very versatile and economical fish. You can buy it in most supermarkets, but it will be far fresher if you get it from a good fishmonger. The Gingerman is supplied by Brighton and Newhaven Fish Sales, which has a retail outlet on Hove Lagoon. For this recipe, you'll need apple wood smoking chips to hot-smoke the mackerel.

4 mackerel fillets
5 juniper berries
1 tsp black peppercorns
1 rosemary sprig
1 tsp coriander seeds
1 bay leaf
110g demerara sugar
200g rock salt
50-100ml Greek yoghurt
½ lemon
½ bunch dill
100ml vegetable oil
1 cucumber, peeled and cut into half-moons
30g salt

For the wasabi yoghurt

3g wasabi paste
35g Greek yoghurt
20g double cream
juice ½ lemon

For the oyster beignets

4 oysters
50g plain four
50g rice flour
1 teaspoon honey
50ml beer
50ml soda water
3 litres vegetable oil (or enough to fill a deep-fat fryer or ¾ fill a large pan)

To garnish

shaved radish, micro radish leaf and oyster leaf.

Recipe overleaf

Run a sharp knife down either side of the bones in the middle of the fillets and gently pull away; it should come away as one piece. Blend the juniper, peppercorns, rosemary, coriander and bay together and mix well with the sugar and salt to make a dry marinade. Dust the base of a shallow baking tray evenly with the marinade and place the fillets on top, then cover with more of the marinade. Cure for 30 mins in the fridge, then wash the fillets under cold running water and dry on kitchen paper. Cut 2 of the fillets into 1cm thick slices, then into cubes and refrigerate until needed. Reserve the other 2 for hot smoking.

To hot-smoke the mackerel, put some apple wood smoking chips in a deep baking tray lined with foil. Put the mackerel fillets on a cooling rack covered with foil. Put the rack into the tray and cover with a lid or foil. Put over a medium heat and smoke the fish for 5 mins. Remove from the heat and allow to cool.

To make a smoked mackerel pâté, flake the fillets into a bowl and add enough Greek yoghurt to bind. Squeeze in the lemon juice and add salt to taste. Chop 1 tbsp of the dill, stir it in and refrigerate until needed.

Chop the remaining dill, add to a pan with the oil and warm to 50°C (use as heat probe or kitchen thermometer to check the temperature). Strain through a fine mesh sieve and allow to cool.

Cure the cucumber in the salt for 1 hr, then wash under running water in a colander before drying on kitchen paper. Marinate the cucumber with the dill oil in a container until needed.

To make the wasabi yoghurt, combine the wasabi and yoghurt in a bowl. Whisk the cream to soft peaks and fold into the yoghurt mixture. Stir in the lemon juice to taste and season with salt.

To make the oyster beignets, heat the oil in a deep-fat fryer to 180°C. Steam the oysters for 3 mins, allow to cool and remove from the shells. Make a tempura batter by mixing the flours together in a bowl. Add the honey, then gradually whisk in the beer and soda water to make a smooth batter. Dip the oysters in the batter and deep fry until golden and crisp. Season with salt.

To serve, put 2 small quenelles of the pâté at right angles on the centre of 4 serving plates. Arrange 3 pieces of cucumber and 6 pieces of cured mackerel around. Spoon some of the dill oil around and dot the plate with the yoghurt. Arrange some of the radish, micro radish leaves and oyster leaves around and serve. At the restaurant, the dish is additionally garnished with a sesame tuile.

Cod with truffle pomme purée and red wine sauce

(Serves 4)

A rich, indulgent dish, you can simplify the preparation by substituting beef or chicken stock for the demi-glace (a heavily reduced veal stock) in the sauce.

Check the cod for any pin bones, remove the skin and refrigerate until needed.

Heat oven to 180°C. Bake 4 of the potatoes in their skins for 1 hr or until soft. Scoop out the flesh and blend in a stand mixer with the cream, milk and butter. Stir in the truffle paste and keep warm.

Cut the leeks in half lengthways, blanch in boiling, salted water for 1 min then refresh in iced water.

Reserve some of the chives for the garnish, then heat the rest in a pan with 100ml of the oil to 50°C (use as heat probe or kitchen thermometer to check the temperature). Strain through a fine mesh sieve into a bowl and allow to cool.

To make the sauce, caramelise the leek, garlic, rosemary, onion and shallot in a large pan. Add the bones and cook for 2 mins. Add the red wine and star anise and reduce by one-third. Add the demi-glace or stock and simmer for 20 mins, then strain through a fine mesh sieve into a clean pan.

Heat the oil in a deep-fat fryer to 190°C. Grate the remaining potato, squeeze out the moisture in a clean tea towel and deep fry for 2-3 mins or until golden brown. Drain on kitchen paper.

Oil the leeks and place cut-side down in a dry, hot pan until charred on all sides. Dress with a squeeze of lemon juice, salt and chive oil to taste.

Gently dust the cod fillets with flour, place in a hot pan with 1 tbsp vegetable oil and cook for 2 mins. Turn the fish over and cook for 2 mins more. Be careful not to overcook the fish otherwise it will begin to flake and collapse. Squeeze over lemon juice and salt to finish.

To serve, divide the pomme purée between 4 plates and top with a piece of cod. Scatter over some of the fried potato, bacon and chives and grate over some truffle. Spoon the red wine sauce and chive oil around the dish and finish with a piece of leek.

4 x 200g cod fillets
5 large Maris Piper potatoes
75ml double cream
75ml milk
150g butter
1 tbsp truffle paste
2 baby leeks
1 bunch chives, finely chopped
100ml vegetable oil, plus more for frying

For the red wine sauce

1 leek, chopped
1 garlic clove, chopped
1 rosemary sprig
½ onion, finely sliced
1 shallot, finely sliced
250g fish bones, washed and chopped
½ bottle red wine
1 star anise
500ml demi-glace or meat stock

To serve

3 litres vegetable oil (or enough to fill a deep-fat fryer or ¾ fill a large pan)
juice 1 lemon
plain flour, for dusting
40g smoked bacon, finely chopped and fried until crisp
1 fresh truffle, for grating

For the confit potato

4 Maris Piper potatoes, cut into 1cm slices
500g duck or beef fat
2 thyme sprigs
2 garlic cloves, crushed

For the pea purée

375g bag frozen peas

For the truffle sauce

200ml sweet wine
200ml white wine
400ml chicken stock
200ml demi-glace or beef stock
250ml whipping cream
1 tsp truffle oil
2 tsp truffle paste

For the asparagus

4 spears white asparagus
4 spears green asparagus
1 star anise
1 juniper berry
1 bay leaf
2 cardamom pods
2 thyme sprigs
1 rosemary sprig

For the beef

4 x 150g beef fillets
1 tbsp vegetable oil
40g butter
2 thyme sprigs
1 rosemary sprig

For the foie gras

200g foie gras
150g plain flour
150g panko breadcrumbs
3 litres vegetable oil (or enough to fill a deep-fat fryer or ¾ fill a large pan)

To serve

100g fresh peas, podded and blanched for 2 mins

Aged beef fillet, foie gras, asparagus

(Serves 4)

Beef accompanied by the best of summer on a plate; you don't have to do much to any of these ingredients when they're at their best. Omit the foie gras if you prefer.

Season the potatoes with salt and pepper. Melt the fat in a pan with the thyme and garlic, add the potatoes and gently cook until the tip of your knife goes in without any resistance. Remove from the fat, allow to cool and trim into neat rounds with a cookie cutter. Reserve.

To make the pea purée, bring a pan water to the boil with plenty of salt and cook the peas for 3-4 mins. Drain and blend until smooth. Push through a fine mesh sieve, allow to cool and refrigerate until needed.

To make the sauce, reduce the wines, stock and demi-glace or beef stock to a glaze, then stir in the cream, truffle oil and paste. Season to taste.

Trim the asparagus. Put the star anise, juniper, bay leaf, cardamom, thyme and rosemary in a pan, cover with water and bring to the boil. Add a little salt, reduce the heat to a simmer and poach the asparagus for 4 mins or until tender. They should retain a slight bite.

Heat oven to 220°C. Caramelise the beef in the oil on all sides in a hot pan. Add the butter, thyme and rosemary and baste the meat well. Transfer to the oven and roast for 3-4 mins for medium-rare, or your liking. Allow to rest for 5-10 mins.

Meanwhile, heat the oil in the deep-fat fryer to 180°C. Cut the foie gras into bite-size pieces and season with salt and pepper. Mix the flour with water in a bowl to make a paste, then add more water until you achieve a coating consistency. Put the panko breadcrumbs in a separate bowl. Coat the foie gras in the flour and water mix, then the breadcrumbs, then deep-fry until golden.

To serve, fry the potatoes in a pan with some of the confit fat until crisp. Re-heat the pea purée. Carve the fillets and lay in the centre of the plate, arrange 1 potato, 1 piece of foie gras, 1 green asparagus spear, 1 white asparagus spear and some of the peas around and spoon over some of the sauce.

Dark chocolate pavé, popcorn ice cream

(Serves 4)

At The Gingerman, we use Valrhona chocolate for this indulgent dessert, but any good-quality dark cooking chocolate will work. This dish needs to be started one day in advance.

For the pavé

95g caster sugar
30ml water
2 egg yolks
1 whole egg
190ml double cream
75g dark chocolate

For the chocolate streusel

22g soft butter
22g demerara sugar
22g ground almonds
17g plain flour
4g cocoa powder

For the popcorn ice cream

230ml full-fat milk
230ml double cream
6 egg yolks
85g caster sugar
50g popcorn

To make the pavé, bring the sugar and water to 121°C in a pan to make a syrup (use a heat probe or kitchen thermometer to check the temperature). Put the yolks and whole egg into a bowl over a bain marie and whisk until doubled in volume. Add the sugar syrup, whisking vigorously for 10 mins to make a sabayon.

Whip the double cream to soft peaks and set aside. Melt the chocolate in a bowl over a bain marie to blood temperature, then fold into the sabayon in 2 equal stages. Fold in the cream, then pour into a baking tray lined with cling film and set in the fridge for a minimum of 6 hrs or preferably overnight.

To make the streusel, heat oven to 170°C. Mix together all the ingredients with a pinch of salt to form a dough. Roll out between 2 sheets of baking parchment and bake for 10 mins. Allow to cool, then place on top of the pavé. Cut into 4 squares.

To make the ice cream, bring the milk and cream to the boil. Whisk the yolks and sugar together, then add to the milk and cream, whisking continuously until you reach 85°C (use a heat probe or kitchen thermometer to check the temperature). Add the popcorn and leave to infuse overnight in the fridge. Churn in an ice-cream machine and freeze.

Serve a piece of the pavé, streusel-side down, with a scoop of the ice cream per person. At the restaurant, the pavé is also served with a blood orange gel and crushed popcorn.

Pecan and white chocolate cannoli

(Serves 4)

A stunning dessert that takes a little effort and organisation. You can buy pear purée online or make your own by cooking peeled, diced pear in a little water before blending.

For the pecan mousse

195ml double cream
50g candied crushed pecans
25g white chocolate
one-third gelatine leaf, soaked in water and drained

To make the mousse, bring 65ml cream to the boil, pour over the nuts, chocolate and gelatine in a mixing bowl and combine well. Cool to 37°C (use a heat probe or kitchen thermometer to check the temperature). Whip the remaining cream to soft peaks and fold into the mix. Pipe into a long thick cylinder onto a tray and freeze.

For the pear jelly

10g pear purée
0.7g agar agar

Make the jelly by heating the purée and agar agar to 90°C for 5 mins (use a heat probe or kitchen thermometer to check the temperature). Pour onto a tray and allow to set. Place the frozen mousse on top of the set jelly and carefully wrap the jelly around the mousse, trimming to shape. Cut the cylinder into 4 equal portions and refrigerate until needed.

For the maple syrup caramel

30g sugar
10ml water
125ml maple syrup

To make the maple syrup caramel, dissolve the sugar in the water in a pan and cook to make a clear caramel, then stir in the maple syrup.

For the poached pear

500ml sugar
500ml water
1 pear, peeled

To poach the pear, dissolve the sugar in the water in a pan to make a simple syrup. Add the pear and poach until soft. Remove the pear and dice into small cubes, reserving 100ml of the syrup for the sorbet.

For the pear sorbet

500g pear purée
100ml syrup from the poached pears

To make the sorbet, mix the purée and 100ml poaching syrup together, churn in an ice cream maker and freeze.

To serve, put a small mound of diced pear onto 4 plates and top with a scoop of the sorbet. Place 1 cannoli alongside and drizzle with maple syrup caramel. At the restaurant, the cannoli is served on top of chopped candied pecans.

Terre à Terre is the grand dame of Brighton's modern restaurant scene and has been serving cutting-edge vegetarian food for more than two decades. Founded by Amanda Powley and Philip Taylor in 1993, the restaurant has grown from humble origins as a small café to serving hundreds of customers every week in the heart of Brighton's Lanes.

Terre à Terre might literally mean 'close to the ground' but the restaurant continually reaches for gastronomic heights; it was Best Restaurant runner-up in the 2016 Observer Food Awards, described by the late AA Gill as 'singularly and eccentrically marvellous' and is rated highly in all the restaurant guides, including 5 out of 5 for 'exceptional food' from the Harden's Guide.

After travelling, cooking and eating their way around the world, Powley and Taylor's paths crossed while working in a vegetarian restaurant in the Lanes. With a burning desire to alter perceptions of vegetarian cooking, partly fuelled by deep-rooted concerns over animal welfare, they decided to open their own restaurant. They found a three-storey dilapidated premises in Pool Valley, just off Brighton's seafront, and carried out the renovations themselves.

The restaurant quickly gained a following for its exuberant, generous and original cooking, including inventive ways with rosti potatoes and a fried rice pudding. Today, after moving to its substantially larger East Street location, the menu continues to take inspiration from around the globe, be it the Middle East or Asia in singularly named dishes such as Souper Dukka and Sneaky Peeking Steamers.

In Autumn 2016, Judith Lang (pictured right) was appointed head chef of the restaurant. "I was working at Toasted in East Dulwich which was very meat focused. I became vegetarian and Terre à Terre was the place I wanted to be," says Sunderland-born Lang, who studied Modern History at Oxford before embarking on a career in the professional kitchen, beginning at Jesmond Dene House in Newcastle.

"It's a very collaborative effort here, Amanda and Phil both have a lot of influence on what we're doing. Everyone brings ideas to the table and we discuss it as a team," says Lang who has recently introduced a new dish, Aloo Sailor, to the menu. "It's a take on sag aloo. It makes vegetables shine when you treat them with respect, but uses all the spices and herbs we have available to elevate them."

Terre à Terre

Terre à Terre

1 cauliflower, cut into florets
350g caster sugar
90ml liquid glucose
100ml tamari
100ml Chinese vinegar
50g white miso
1 tbsp finely chopped chilli
1 tbsp finely chopped root ginger
2 tbsp finely chopped garlic
2 tsp ground Sichuan pepper
1 star anise
3 litres vegetable oil (or enough to fill a deep-fat fryer or ¾ fill a large pan)
2 tbsp mixed black and white sesame seeds

For the batter

15g xantham gum
120g rice flour
1 tsp salt

For the chestnut purée

100g shallots, sliced
1 tsp vegetable oil
250g ready-cooked chestnuts, peeled and sliced
30ml white wine
2 tsp lemon juice

Korean fried cauliflower

(Serves 4)

At the restaurant, this vegan-friendly, gluten-free take on the famous takeaway food is served with pickled mouli, kale crisps, an onigiri rice ball and pickled ginger gel - but here the recipe has been simplified for home cooks.

Bring a large pan of salted water to the boil and blanch the florets for 3 mins. Refresh in iced water, then drain and dry.

To prepare the glaze, combine the sugar and glucose with 75ml water in a heavy- bottom pan. Whisk over a medium heat until the sugar dissolves. Increase the heat to high and boil until the mix reaches 120°C. Add the tamari, vinegar, miso, chilli, ginger, garlic, Sichuan pepper and star anise and cook on a low heat for 1 hr until sticky and full of flavour. Strain through a fine mesh sieve.

To make the batter, use a hand blender to thoroughly combine the xantham gum with 500ml water. Add the flour and salt and continue blending until a smooth batter is formed.

To make the chestnut purée, sweat the shallots in the oil until soft and translucent. Add the sliced chestnuts and wine. Allow the wine to reduce, then add 300ml water and cook on a low heat until everything is soft. Blend until very smooth and push through a fine mesh sieve. Stir in the lemon juice to taste.

To serve, heat the oil in a deep-fat fryer to 180°C. Dip the cauliflower into the batter until well-coated and fry for 5 mins or until the batter is fully cooked and crunchy. Drain on kitchen paper, then dip each piece into the glaze and then into sesame seeds. Place some of the warmed purée on 4 plates and sit the cauliflower pieces on top.

A filo pastry tower is removed to reveal the blue cheese soufflé inside, recipe overleaf

For the blue cheese soufflé

50g butter, plus more for coating
60g plain flour, plus more for coating
250ml warmed milk
1 tsp Dijon mustard
125g Brighton Blue cheese
5 large eggs

For the wrap

12 sheets filo pastry
65g butter, melted
30g sumac powder

For the apple tattie pavé pie

1kg Desirée potatoes, thinly sliced
2 large cooking apples, peeled, cored and thinly
sliced
2 onions, thinly sliced
500ml vegetable stock

For the Jerusalem artichoke purée

400g Jerusalem artichokes, peeled and sliced
150ml full-fat milk
1 pinch mace

For the Sussex Charmer sauce

300ml whipping cream, plus a little extra for
the purée
200g Sussex Charmer cheese
1 pinch nutmeg

Chimchimney soufflé and sooty tops

(Serves 6)

This dish is a celebration of Sussex cheese and features mellow, aromatic Brighton Blue from High Weald Dairy in Horsted Keynes and Sussex Charmer, a unique cross between Cheddar and Parmesan made in Rudgwick.

Coat the inside of six 100ml soufflé ramekins with soft butter and then a little flour. Melt the 50g butter in a pan over a low heat. Sprinkle in the flour and stir to combine, then gently cook over a medium heat, stirring constantly. Take off the heat and slowly pour in the warmed milk while whisking. Cook the mix on a low heat until it's smooth and thick. Add the mustard and cheese, and stir until melted. Take the pan off the heat.

Separate the eggs and beat in 4 of the yolks (save the 5th yolk for another recipe). Allow the mix to cool fully. Heat oven to 180°C. In another bowl, whip up all the egg whites until stiff peaks form and gently fold into the cheese mix. Divide between the ramekins and cook in the oven in a deep tray with enough water to come halfway up the ramekins for 15-20 mins or until risen and slightly golden. Remove from the ramekins and chill until required.

To wrap the soufflés, place one sheet of filo on a dry surface, brush lightly with melted butter and dust with sumac. Place the second sheet directly on top and again brush with butter and dust with sumac, working swiftly to prevent the pastry sheets from drying out.

Flip the pastry sandwich over so it's buttered-side down, then fold the top edge down just past the middle of the sheets and fold the bottom edge up to just overlap it. Jus-Rol filo, which comes in packs of 6 sheets, is recommended for this dish. If using, at this point, cut the pastry in half vertically so that each half will wrap one soufflé (roughly 250mm x 100mm for each wrapper).

Place the soufflé on its side on the bottom edge of the wrapper and gently roll it up, sealing the join with a little of the melted butter and some gentle persuasion. Stand them upright on a baking sheet and refrigerate well for a minimum of 1 hr. This is vital as it ensures that the pastry sides remain upright during cooking.

To make the pie, heat oven to 180°C. Line a baking dish with baking parchment. Layer the potatoes, apples and onions, seasoning each layer. Add enough of the stock to cover the ingredients, then cover the dish with a layer of parchment. Bake for 30 mins or until a knife can be inserted without resistance. Press (cut a piece of cardboard to fit the dish, cover with tin foil and use tinned food to weigh it down) and refrigerate.

For the artichoke purée, simmer the artichokes in the milk and mace in a pan until very soft. Blend until smooth, push through a fine mesh sieve into a clean pan and finish with a splash of cream.

To make the cheese sauce, bring the cream to the boil, then add the cheese. Take off the heat and stir until the cheese has melted and the sauce is smooth. Add the nutmeg and black pepper to taste.

To serve, cut a portion of the pie and reheat in the oven with the soufflé at 180°C for 15 mins or until the pastry is brown and the soufflé hot and risen. Spoon the reheated artichoke purée onto 6 plates, place a soufflé on top and cover with a pastry wrap, spoon in some of the cheese sauce and finish with a piece of pie alongside. Optionally, serve as at the restaurant with pickled vegetables, sauerkraut and fried sage leaves as per the photograph. Your guests can lift the pastry wrap to reveal the soufflé inside.

For the Yemen paste

230g hot red chilli peppers, chopped
5 garlic cloves
¼ tbsp black peppercorns
½ tsp coriander seeds
65g coriander (leaves and stalks)
½ tsp salt
150ml olive oil, plus extra for topping up

For the lemony Yemeni pickle

3 lemons, peel and pith removed, segmented
100ml lemon juice
peel 3 preserved lemons
150g caster sugar

For the sea salad tartare sauce

1 nori sheet (dried seaweed)
150ml mayonnaise
40g finely chopped parsley
100g capers, rinsed and finely chopped
100g gherkins, rinsed and finely chopped
100g Thai pink shallots, finely chopped

For the chip shop batter

150g plain flour
75g self-raising flour
10ml white wine vinegar
240ml cold water
½ tsp baking powder

For the buttermilk-soaked halloumi

500g halloumi, cut into thin triangles
500ml buttermilk
plain flour, for coating
3 litres vegetable oil (or enough to fill a deep-fat
fryer or ¾ fill a large pan

For the minty mushy peas

400g fresh or frozen peas
40g mint, leaves chopped, stalks reserved
40g parsley, leaves chopped, stalks reserved
50g unsalted butter

To serve

1 lemon, cut into quarters and griddled
2 tbsp chopped mint
3 pickled quail's eggs, halved

Better batter and lemony Yemeni relish

(Serves 4-6)

A fitting tribute to the 'kiss me quick' kitsch Brighton seaside, this dish was dreamt up over a mug of tea in the early years of the restaurant, making it a Terre à Terre classic.

To make the Yemen paste, blend the ingredients together. Make the pickle by blending half the lemon segments, juice and preserved lemon peel together. Put in a small pan with the sugar, stir and heat gently. Boil rapidly for 2 mins. Add ½ tsp of the Yemen paste or according to taste. Leave to cool, then add the remaining lemon segments.

Make the tartare sauce by briefly scorching the nori over a flame on both sides for no more than 2 secs or it will burn. Crumble into the mayonnaise and stir in the parsley, capers, gherkins and shallots.

To make the batter, whisk all the ingredients together to the consistency of double cream. Refrigerate until needed.

Submerge the halloumi in the buttermilk and leave to soak in the fridge for several hours or overnight.

To make the mushy peas, cook the peas with the herb stalks in boiling water until tender. Drain well, discarding the stalks. Blend the peas with the butter and chopped herbs, seasoning to taste.

To serve, heat a deep-fat fryer to 180ºC. Drain the halloumi, dip in plain flour and then in the batter. Deep-fry, 2 pieces at a time, until crisp and golden brown. Drain on kitchen paper.

Divide the halloumi between 4-6 plates and top with a spoonful of the pickle. Add the re-heated mushy peas. Finish with the sea salad tartare, and garnish with a griddled lemon quarter, chopped mint and half a pickled quail's egg.

Churrosimo

(Serves 6-8)

This vegan-friendly dessert dates back centuries to Spanish shepherds who developed a sweet stick that could be easily cooked in a pan over an open fire in the mountains. They taste even better by the sea.

500g strong flour
¼ tsp salt
½ tsp caster sugar
50g soya margarine
5g dried yeast
280ml warm water
½ tsp ground cinnamon
40g caster sugar
3 litres vegetable oil (or enough to fill a deep-fat fryer or ¾ fill a large pan)

For the vodka cherries

300g fresh cherries, stoned
200ml vodka
1-2 tsp runny honey (optional)

For the chocolate dip

250g dark chocolate (70% cocoa solids), broken into pieces
300ml soya cream
2 tbsp hot water

For the salt caramel dip

300g granulated sugar
300ml soya cream
pinch sea salt

To make the churros, sift the flour, salt and sugar together into a bowl and rub in the margarine. Stir the yeast into the warm water, make a well in the flour and pour in the yeast. Mix to a smooth dough either by hand or with a hook attachment on a stand mixer. Once the dough has formed, knead for 5-6 mins.

Cut into quarters, cover with a damp cloth and leave for 5 mins to allow the dough to puff up slightly. Divide each quarter into 3 pieces and roll each one into a 10cm long cigar shape. Place the churros on a lined baking tray, cover loosely with cling film and allow to prove for 1 hr. They do not need to double in size as they will expand when they are being fried (the churros can be frozen at this point. Defrost for 1 hr before cooking).

Cover the cherries in vodka (add more if you dare), cover with cling film and leave to macerate overnight. Add a small amount of honey if you prefer things a little sweeter and refrigerate until needed.

Prepare the cinnamon sugar by mixing the cinnamon into the sugar.

Make the chocolate dip by putting the chocolate into a medium sized bowl. Bring the soya cream to the boil, pour onto the chocolate and stir with a small balloon whisk until thoroughly combined. Stir in the hot water.

To make the salt caramel dip, bring the sugar to the boil and cook until light brown. Off the heat, whisk in the soya cream, using a long-handled whisk to avoid splashing your hands with the hot caramel. Add the salt and leave to cool.

To serve, heat a deep-fat fryer to 180°C. Deep-fry the churros for 2-3 mins, or shallow fry them (turning regularly) until golden all over. While they are still hot, roll them in the cinnamon sugar. Set the bowl of chocolate dip over a pan of simmering water and warm through without letting it boil, then pour into small bowls. Pour the salt caramel dip into bowls. Divide the chilled vodka cherries into cold glasses, adding cocktail sticks for spearing the fruit, and put these with the hot churros onto serving plates.

Bum
(Serves 6)

The name is simply a bit of Brighton end-of-pier humour on the part of the restaurant - who couldn't resist a little bit of Bum? The restaurant uses Sussex Slipcote from High Weald Dairy for this recipe but any mild soft sheep's milk cheese will work.

Pour the Sambuca over the sultanas to cover and leave to macerate at room temperature for 24 hrs.

Make the cheesecake by crumbling the cheese into a bowl and adding the egg and yolks, sugar, vanilla and the zest and juice of the lemon. Mix with a spatula to form a smooth paste, then add the cream in 2 batches until combined. Stir in the soaked sultanas and mix well, leaving a few aside to decorate the cheesecake.

Line six 7.5 x 5cm rings with 15cm squares of greaseproof paper and gently mould them into the rings, taking care not to tear the paper and leaving a slight overhang. Carefully fill the moulds with the cheesecake mix.

Heat oven to 160ºC. Coat the rosemary sprigs in olive oil and push a sprig into the centre of each mould. Place the rings in a deep sided roasting tray and pour in hot water to come three quarters up the sides of the rings. Bake for 20 mins or until set, then remove and cool.

To make the biscotti, heat oven to 180ºC. Put the flour, sugar, star anise, baking powder, citrus zests and fennel seeds in a large mixing bowl and make a well in the centre. Pour in the beaten egg and work together to form a sticky dough. Mix in the walnuts and turn out onto a floured surface. Sprinkle a little flour on top of the dough and roll the mix into a sausage shape about 30cm long. Transfer to a baking sheet lined with baking parchment (don't worry if it breaks, it's easy to stick back together). Bake for 20-25 mins or until golden brown and set. The mix will spread and rise as it cooks.

Remove from the oven, and turn the heat down to 130ºC. Allow the biscotti mixture to cool for 15 mins, then place on a chopping board and gently cut with a serrated knife into 2cm slices. Return the slices to the baking sheet and dry out in the oven for 20 mins. Cool and store in an airtight container. The biscuits will keep for a couple of weeks.

To serve, remove the rings from the cheesecakes, carefully peel off the greaseproof paper and place on serving plates with some of the sultanas and a couple of warm biscotti (they can be heated gently at 180ºC for a few mins). At the restaurant, we serve this with lemon and rosemary-infused syrup, grapes and candied rosemary.

For the Sambuca sultanas

45ml Sambuca
100g sultanas

For the cheesecake

400g soft sheep's milk cheese
1 egg and 3 yolks, beaten
50g caster sugar
½ tsp vanilla extract
zest and juice 1 lemon
400ml double cream
6 rosemary sprigs
2 tsp olive oil

For the almond fennel biscotti

200g plain flour, plus extra for rolling
200g caster sugar
½ tsp ground star anise
1 tsp baking powder
grated zest 1 orange
grated zest 1 lemon
grated zest 2 limes
½ tsp fennel seeds
2 eggs and 2 yolks, beaten
150g walnuts, roughly chopped

Curry Leaf Café

The orange and green colours of Curry Leaf Café are a common sight around Brighton. Chef Kanthi Thamma (pictured right centre) and business partner, journalist Euan Sey opened the original café in 2014 in the Lanes serving dishes inspired by Thamma's home city of Hyderabad in Southern India, and made with Sussex produce. The duo then launched a street food kiosk at Brighton station offering pakoras, samosas and bhajis (as well as wicked vindaloo bacon rolls) and, most recently, opened Kemptown Kitchen serving Indian small plates and street food.

Thamma began his career at the Taj Fort Aguada in Goa, where he worked in India's first Italian restaurant. After a stint in Switzerland, Thamma moved to Florida to work for Walt Disney World Resorts and Disney Cruise Line, then took a position at the Imperial Hotel in Torquay.

"I landed in the UK ten years ago with the dream of opening an Indian restaurant, but not knowing where or when. Brighton was an accident. I was given a hotel voucher by the Imperial for Christmas. I tried to book a couple of hotels but they were full, so the Old Ship in Brighton was the third choice. It was love at first sight. I found The Chilli Pickle by chance and ate my lunch there, it was just amazing."

Thamma ended up working for Alun Sperring at The Chilli Pickle and it was during that time he answered Sey's advert on Gumtree for a flatmate. "I kept talking about my concept for Curry Leaf Café. His passion for good food, and the trust he had in me after trying my cooking, made him jump into the business without any previous experience. After six months we started looking for a premises in Brighton."

The restaurant quickly found favour with best-selling dishes like Tandoor-grilled Hyderabadi lamb chops and - Thamma's personal favourite - battered and deep-fried Guntur Chilli Bhajis. "I have many childhood memories attached to these recipes. They show how a simple street-side vegetarian snack can be packed with flavour and textures."

Thamma has already exceeded his dream of opening a small café serving South Indian food with events, pop-ups and collaborations, as well as awards and a following for the three Curry Leaf outlets. But he's not done yet. "One day I would love to see Curry Leaf Cafés spread across Europe".

Curry Leaf Café

Southern fried chicken

(Serves 4)

This is a simple yet delicious chicken street-food snack from South India that chef Thamma grew up eating. It also works great as a bite to go with a beer or two.

10g coriander seeds
10g cumin seeds
1 star anise
2 cloves
5g fennel seeds
50g rice flour
25g cornflour
50g ginger, ground to a paste
50g garlic, ground to a paste
15ml lime juice
20g red chilli powder
½ tsp turmeric
½ tsp salt
10 fresh curry leaves, chopped, plus extra to garnish
500g boneless chicken thighs, each cut into 4 pieces
3 litres vegetable oil (or enough to fill a deep-fat fryer or ¾ fill a large pan)
1 onion, sliced
4 lime wedges

Grind the coriander, cumin, star anise, cloves and fennel together to make a spice mix. Put in a bowl with the rice flour, cornflour, ginger and garlic pastes, lime juice, chilli powder, turmeric, salt and curry leaves and mix well to make a thick paste. Add the chicken and leave to marinate for 30 mins.

Heat the oil in a deep-fat fryer to 180°C (or in a deep pan), and carefully drop in the chicken pieces. Fry for 3 mins or until cooked (if in doubt, take one piece out and cut in half to check). Drain on kitchen paper and serve hot with the sliced onion, curry leaves and lime wedges.

Keralan mussel moilee

(Serves 4)

Easy, quick to cook and packed with flavour, moilee is a Keralan dish from the Syrian Christian community and is believed to have been created by the Portuguese during the time of colonisation. A fragrant and spicy stew with coconut milk as a base, it's often cooked with fish or prawns but here is combined with mussels, a personal favourite of chef Thamma.

1kg mussels
100g coconut oil
5g mustard seeds
2g fenugreek seeds
10 green cardamom pods
1 blade of mace
15 cloves
10g cinnamon stick
10 curry leaves
100g root ginger, cut into julienne
10 garlic cloves, sliced
2 green chillies, halved
2 medium white onions, sliced
½ tsp turmeric
250ml thick coconut milk
1 small bunch salad fennel

Clean the mussels in plenty of cold water, removing the beards and scraping any barnacles off the shells with a knife. Heat the coconut oil in a pan over a low heat. Add the mustard and fenugreek and cook until the seeds start to pop. Add the cardamom, mace, cloves, cinnamon and curry leaves, sauté for 1 min, then add the ginger, garlic, chillies and onions. Stir for 3-4 mins making sure the spices do not burn. Add the turmeric and coconut milk, simmer for 5 mins and season with salt.

Put the cleaned mussels in a separate pan on a medium flame, cover with a lid and allow to steam for 2 mins or until they open. Add the moilee sauce, cover and cook for another 2 mins. Adjust the seasoning if necessary before serving in 4 hot bowls garnished with the salad fennel.

Curry Leaf Café

Baked hara chutney mackerel

(Serves 4)

Hara chutney, made of green herbs like coriander and mint, is traditionally served with tandoor dishes in India but here it's used to marinate whole baked fish. This will work with all types of fish but goes particularly well with mackerel.

4 whole mackerel (about 125g each)
2 bunches coriander
1 bunch mint
50g root ginger, peeled
6 garlic cloves, peeled
4 green chillies
50ml lime juice
1 mango
50g shallots, chopped
1 red chilli, finely chopped

Heat oven to 180°C. Clean the mackerel, remove the heads (leave the tail on for presentation) and score on both sides. Blend 1 bunch coriander with the mint, ginger, garlic, chillies and lime juice to a thick paste and rub into the fish on both sides. Bake for 6 mins.

Make the mango salsa by slicing the mango either side of the central stone so that you have two cheeks of flesh. Chop one into small dice and blend the other to a purée (use 2 tbsp of ready-made mango purée if the mango is not ripe enough to blend). Pick the leaves from 2 of the coriander stalks and chop roughly. Combine the diced and puréed mango in a bowl with the shallots, chilli and coriander and add to the mango pulp.

Serve one mackerel per person with the salsa spooned over and some of the remaining coriander to garnish.

Sweetcorn and green pea vadas

(Serves 4)

This vegan dish is inspired by masala vada, the famous South Indian street food. Usually made with lentils, this recipe uses sweetcorn and green peas, two commonly-used freezer ingredients that can quickly be converted into a tasty snack - just defrost before using. The vadas are usually deep fried but can be pan fried, just make sure you use a non-stick pan and enough oil so they don't stick.

For the tomato ginger chutney

2 tomatoes
25g ginger
6 garlic cloves, peeled
1 red chilli
20ml vegetable oil
½ bunch coriander

For the vadas

200g sweetcorn kernels
200g green peas
10g green chillies, chopped
50g root ginger, peeled and chopped
leaves from 5 coriander stalks
10g fennel seeds
65g rice flour
3 litres vegetable oil (or enough to fill a deep-fat fryer or ¾ fill a large pan)

Heat oven to 180°C. To make the chutney, put the tomatoes, ginger, garlic and chilli in a roasting pan and coat with the oil. Roast for 6-7 mins, allow to cool then blend with the coriander until smooth.

Heat the oil in a deep-fat fryer or large pan to 180°C. Coarsely blend the sweetcorn and peas (you don't want a fine paste). In a bowl, combine with the chilli, ginger, coriander and fennel seeds. Season to taste with salt. Add the rice flour and mix well. Divide into 16 portions and flatten gently between your palms. Deep fry until golden brown and serve hot with the chutney.

Butternut payasam

(Serves 4)

Payasam is a traditional dessert from South India served during festivals and special occasions. It's generally made with milk but this version is dairy-free, using coconut milk. Using vegetables in India to make sweets and desserts is common practice (carrot halwa is a great example) and here, the butternut squash - substituted for the more usual rice or vermicelli - adds some distinctive sweetness and texture.

500g butternut squash, cut into small dice
250ml coconut milk
100g jaggery, palm sugar or brown sugar
¼ tsp ground cardamom
25g coconut oil
10g cashew nuts
10g pistachios

Bring a pan of water to the boil and cook the diced squash for 4-5 mins or until tender. Drain and remove a few pieces (these will be used for garnish), then mash the remainder with the back of a fork. Bring the coconut milk to a gentle simmer in a pan and add the butternut purée, jaggery (or sugar) and ground cardamom. Simmer for 5 mins. In a separate pan, heat the coconut oil and sauté the cashews, pistachios and reserved squash for 1 min. Divide the payasam between 4 bowls, garnish each with some of the nut mixture and serve immediately.

Hidden away in North Laine, in a converted financial advisor's office, is one of Brighton's most ambitious and exciting restaurants. The intimate Isaac At serves a multi-course tasting menu of carefully honed and beautifully presented dishes created from seasonal Sussex produce, matched with local wines. Heading up the restaurant's youthful, enthusiastic team is 24-year-old chef-patron Isaac Bartlett-Copeland who runs a brigade of three chefs in the small open kitchen with quiet assurance and purpose.

"I want to make the restaurant one of the best in the South," says Bartlett-Copeland (pictured right) who launched Isaac At in early 2015 as a sort of permanent pop-up, opening for dinner on Fridays and Saturdays only. An immediate success, the restaurant received numerous positive write-ups and just over a year later, Bartlett-Copeland renovated and re-launched Isaac At as a full-time operation.

Despite his youth, Bartlett-Copeland managed to pack in a lot of culinary experience before opening his own place at just 22 (making him the youngest head chef and restaurateur in the country). He grew up in Lewes cooking with his uncle, a former head pastry chef of The Ritz and Harrods, and was washing pots in a local pub when he was 15. A year later, he joined the brigade at Brighton's Grand Hotel working under head chef Alan White and, after a short stint at Deans Place Hotel in Alfriston, headed to London.

There, Bartlett-Copeland amassed a wealth of experience working at The Ritz, Restaurant Tom Aikens and The Harwood Arms, and completed more than a dozen one-day trials at restaurants such as L'Autre Pied. "I realised that I could learn so much in 16 hours working somewhere on a trial basis. I wanted to make sure I knew enough to be able to open my own place. I felt that if I went and did my own thing I'd be able to progress better because there'd be no restrictions and I could do what I wanted to do."

Bartlett-Copeland cites meals at Restaurant Sat Bains in Nottingham, Noma in Copenhagen and New York's Eleven Madison Park as influential and formative experiences. "When you think back to an incredible meal, you often just remember one thing on a dish and that's what we're really trying to work on - just taking one or two flavours and making them the best we can."

Isaac At

Roasted cauliflower and wild garlic

(Serves 4)

This dish showcases the fantastic cauliflower that Isaac At sources from Henfield in Sussex. Many of the restaurant's customers who have tried the dish say that it's hard to believe it's just cauliflower. Three-cornered wild garlic is available in the spring, ask a keen forager to find you some.

200ml white wine vinegar
140g caster sugar
8 fresh walnuts
100g butter
2 cauliflowers
2 Bramley apples
juice 1 lemon
1 handful of hay
12 stalks three-cornered wild garlic

Three days ahead, make a pickling solution by combining the vinegar with 100g sugar in a bowl. Crack the walnuts and submerge in the solution. Cover the bowl and refrigerate until needed.

Heat 50g butter in a pan until it foams and turns a golden colour. Remove from the heat. Finely slice one cauliflower and cook in vigorously boiling water for 4 mins; it should remain slightly undercooked. Put in a blender with the golden butter and blitz to a purée.

Peel the apples and put the peel in a bowl of water and lemon juice to prevent browning, then refrigerate. Put the apples in a large saucepan with a handful of hay. Light the hay and cover with a lid immediately, trapping as much smoke inside the pan as possible. Leave the apple to smoke for 15 mins, then core and finely slice. Add to a pan with the remaining sugar and cook until very soft. Blend to a purée, then cool in the fridge. Return to the blender, add the peel and blitz again before pushing through a fine sieve. Refrigerate until needed.

Heat oven to 180°C. Heat the remaining butter in a hot pan, slice the remaining cauliflower into 8 wedges and cook, cut-face down, until browned. Transfer to the oven for 8 mins or until just soft.

To serve, gently reheat the cauliflower purée in a pan. Put a spoonful of this onto 4 plates and hit the purée with the back of the spoon so that it splatters (this will give your plate visual impact and impress your guests. Wear an apron!) Place 2 pieces of roasted cauliflower on top of the purée and garnish with drops of apple purée, some of the pickled walnuts that you have roughly chopped and finish with 3 stalks of wild garlic.

Pollock, Jerusalem artichoke and nasturtium

(Serves 4)

Pollock is a member of the cod family and is a sustainable and affordable alternative to its larger relative. It pairs fantastically well with the earthy and caramelised flavours of the Jerusalem artichoke in this recipe. You will have some of the artichoke puree leftover which goes well with other white fish or roast meats. The dish is garnished with edible Nasturtium flowers so find a garden fanatic friend that can source you some.

500g pollock fillet, pin-boned and skinned
1-2 tbsp rock salt
600g Jerusalem artichokes
50g butter
nasturtium flowers and extra virgin rapeseed oil, to serve

Generously season the pollock all over with rock salt, wrap tightly in cling film to form a log shape and refrigerate for 3 hrs to allow the salt to draw the moisture from the fish.

Peel 400g Jerusalem artichokes and finely slice using a mandolin or very sharp knife. Heat the butter in a pan, then add the artichokes. Leave on a medium heat to soften and caramelise, stirring every 2 mins to prevent sticking (this is a similar process to caramelising onions). Transfer to a blender and blitz to a smooth purée.

Heat oven to 180°C. Remove the pollock from the fridge and unwrap, discarding any moisture. Slice into 4 even pieces, place on a baking tray lined with greaseproof paper and bake for 4 mins or until cooked through.

Peel and finely slice the remaining Jerusalem artichokes on a mandolin or with a very sharp knife (make sure you do this at the last minute when you're ready to plate the dish, as the flesh will quickly go brown).

Reheat the artichoke purée in a pan. Spread a generous spoonful of the purée with a spatula across 4 serving plates. Place a pollock fillet on each plate and arrange the freshly sliced raw artichoke on top of the fish. Garnish with freshly cut nasturtium leaves and drizzle with extra virgin rapeseed oil.

Veal, smoked broccoli, kohlrabi and purple kale

(Serves 4)

This dish showcases the best of Sussex winter brassica which pair perfectly with the subtle flavour of veal. You'll probably need to order the veal loin in advance from your butcher, who may throw in the bones for the glaze for free.

800g veal loin
1.5kg veal bones, roughly chopped (ask your butcher to do this)
1 tsp cornflour
1 head broccoli
1 tbsp rock salt
wood chips, for smoking
50ml double cream
2 kohlrabi
1 bunch parsley
1 tbsp vegetable oil
125g butter
1 head purple kale

Heat oven to 150°C. Trim the veal of sinew, or ask your butcher to do it for you. Roast the bones for 1½ hrs. Remove from the oven and put in a pan with 2 litres of hot (not boiling) water, then simmer for 8 hrs. Pour through a fine sieve into a clean pan and reduce to 200ml over a high heat. Stir in the cornflour, slaked with a little water, and continue to cook until thickened to a glaze.

Using a pair of scissors, trim the broccoli all over by about 3mm, reserving the trim.
Finely slice the rest of the broccoli. Prepare a large bowl of iced water. Add the rock salt to a large pan of water (it should taste like sea water) and bring to the boil. Add the broccoli and cook for 5 mins (make sure the water continues to boil after you've added the broccoli to retain its fresh colour and flavour). Add the broccoli trim, bring back to the boil, then strain immediately. Plunge into the iced water to retain the colour. Leave to cool for 3 mins, then strain and transfer to a blender. Blitz to a smooth purée.

Put some wood chips in a large pan. Pour the cream into a heatproof bowl and rest it on the wood chips. Light the wood and cover with a lid, trapping as much of the smoke as possible. Leave for 1 hr then mix into the broccoli purée.

Cut the kohlrabi into 5mm slices, then cut discs from the slices with a small cookie cutter, reserving the trim. Place the discs in a vacuum-pack bag, spreading them out into a single layer. Cook in a water bath at 75°C for 20 mins. If you don't have a water bath, pop them into a zip-lock bag and lower carefully into a pan of water, heated to just below boiling point. The water will push the air out of the bag which you can then seal. Cook for 10 mins, making sure the water doesn't boil otherwise the vegetable will overcook.

Blend the leftover kohlrabi trim with the parsley and pass through a sieve. Put the cooked kohlrabi discs in a fresh vacuum-pack bag with the sieved kohlrabi and parsley juice and seal to compress. This technique will add freshness back into the cooked kohlrabi. If you don't have a vac-pack machine, simply combine the cooked kohlrabi with the juice in a bowl and refrigerate until needed.

Heat oven to 180°C. Season the veal with salt and pepper. Heat the vegetable oil in an ovenproof pan to smoking point and sear the meat all over. Roast for 10-15 mins or until the core temperature reaches 48°C (test with a temperature probe). Remove from the oven, add a healthy knob of the butter to the pan and baste. Allow to rest for 5-7 mins, basting from time to time. While the veal is resting, the core temperature should increase to 57-58°C degrees. Carve and season the exposed flesh with salt and pepper.

Put the remaining butter in a large pan with 100ml water, which should be about 1cm deep in the pan. Add the kale stalk down with the leaves above the water so that they steam. Bring to the boil and cook for 10 secs or until tender.

Heat the smoked broccoli purée in a pan, making sure you bring it to the boil for a few secs to bind the broccoli with the cream. Swipe a spoonful of the purée across four serving plates and place 2 slices of veal per portion on top. Drain the kohlrabi on kitchen paper, then scatter around the plates. Place 2 leaves of kale on each plate and drizzle the warmed glaze around to finish.

Sirloin steak, egg yolk and beetroot ketchup

(Serves 4)

This dish is a twist on chef Isaac's favourite beef tartare. The dish uses sirloin rather than fillet which he believes has a better flavour. This recipe will make more beetroot ketchup than you need but it will keep in the fridge and is great in a bacon sandwich. You will need a water bath and a vacuum-pack machine to make this dish.

400g beef sirloin, diced into 0.5cm cubes
4 eggs
1 large banana shallot, thinly sliced into rings
7 cloves
1kg beetroot, peeled and chopped
250ml white wine vinegar
250g sugar
5 pink peppercorns
10 fennel seeds
1 bay leaf
1 cinnamon stick
1g xanthan gum or 1 tsp cornflour
1 cucumber, peeled, de-seeded and diced
2-3 tsp extra virgin rapeseed oil
1 tsp English mustard
radish shoots or mustard cress, to serve

Place the beef in a bowl and refrigerate until needed. Cook the eggs in their shells in a water bath at 64.5°C for 1 hr. Peel and wash off the white, retaining the yolks. Refrigerate until needed.

Make a brine of 100ml water with 3g salt and brine the shallot rings with 5 of the cloves for 4-6 hrs.

Put the beetroot in a large pan with 50ml white wine vinegar, 50g caster sugar and 50ml water. Put the remaining cloves, peppercorns, fennel seeds, bay leaf and cinnamon stick in a piece of muslin cloth, tie into a bag and add to the pan. Bring to the boil, then simmer for 1 hr or until the beetroot is cooked. Stir from time to time and add more water if necessary to ensure the pan doesn't dry out.

Remove the spice bag and blend the beetroot to a smooth consistency. Stir in the xanthan gum (or add the cornflour, slaked with water) to achieve a ketchup consistency. Refrigerate until ready to serve.

Heat the remaining vinegar and sugar together in a pan, then cool. Add the cucumber, then pour the contents of the pan into a vacuum-pack bag and refrigerate until needed (this keeps the cucumber crunchy and retains its shape).

To serve, allow the beef and eggs to come to room temperature. Season the beef with salt and pepper and mix with enough rapeseed oil to coat. Season the yolks with salt and pepper and stir in the mustard to form a purée.

Spread a quarter of the egg yolk purée on each plate, divide the beef between the plates and put some of the cucumber and shallots on top. Decorate with dots of beetroot ketchup and finish with the radish shoots or cress.

Caramelised apple, flapjack and cinnamon ice cream

(Serves 4)

This dish was created to showcase winter Sussex apples and is reminiscent of a classic apple crumble.

A day in advance, mix the egg yolks with 100g sugar. In a pan, bring the milk and cream to the boil with the cinnamon stick, whisking occasionally. Remove the cinnamon and pour onto the egg mixture, whisking constantly. The mix needs to reach between 68-75°C (use a heat probe to check). If necessary, return to a low heat and stir until it reaches the correct temperature. Churn in an ice-cream maker and freeze until needed.

To make the flapjack, heat oven to 180°C. Warm 100g butter with the golden syrup in a pan, then add the oats and mix well. Spread onto a baking tray and bake for 12-15 mins or until golden. Allow to cool slightly, then break into chunks.

Peel 4 of the apples (retaining the skin for the apple pickling liquor) and use a melon baller to scoop apple balls. Place in water with the lemon juice until needed. Finely slice the remaining apple, discarding the core, and put in a pan with 60g sugar and the remaining butter. Stir until the apple is very soft but not caramelised. Blend to a smooth purée.

Blend the apple skins and sieve over a bowl to capture the juice. Heat 10g sugar with the vinegar in a pan until the sugar dissolves. Cool the mixture, then add 40ml of the apple skin juice. Slice the remaining unpeeled apple on a mandolin and place in the pickling liquor for 1-4 hrs, the longer the better.

Drain the apple balls and dry on kitchen paper. Put the remaining sugar into a pan and heat to a golden caramel. Toss the apple balls in the caramel for about 3 mins until they are cooked and coated to create mini toffee apples.

To serve, place chunks of flapjack in a circle in the centre of 4 serving plates. Arrange apple balls around the crumbs and drape the pickled apple over to create a 'cradle'. Place a quenelle of the ice cream on top and serve immediately.

4-6 egg yolks (100g in weight)
370g sugar
400ml milk
100ml double cream
1 cinnamon stick
130g butter
100g golden syrup
200g rolled oats
5 apples (Granny Smith or Braeburn)
juice 1 lemon
10ml white wine vinegar

When Ben McKellar (pictured far right) of The Gingerman fame (see page 140) opened The Ginger Pig in 2006, he introduced the concept of a modern gastropub to the city. With two fine-dining restaurants to his name already in the form of The Gingerman and The Gingerman at Drakes Hotel (now closed), it was time to branch out.

"I like pubs. You can do a really nice foie gras terrine and that can sit alongside something really quite simple. That's what really attracted me to it, because that's how I like to eat," says McKellar, who designs the pub's menus - which include the likes of Guinea fowl breast with parsley gnocchi and ceps - with head chef Tom Wright (pictured right).

"Tom has worked for me for a long time. He started off as sous chef at The Ginger Fox and went on to be head chef at The Ginger Dog. He worked in Australia, then came back to the Pig a couple of years ago," says McKellar. "It's a constant collaboration. Mark chooses the menu and we talk about it, have a tasting session and see what needs to be tweaked, then it goes live. As long as the food is good, I'm happy."

The Brighton scene has changed radically since the Pig opened, something that McKellar is profoundly aware of. Embracing the idea of the city as an emerging foodie destination, he has invested in 11 en-suite bedrooms at the pub, opening in summer 2017, as well as a stunning private dining room. At the time of writing, further developments included expanding the bar area and a brand-new kitchen.

McKellar puts quality above locality, but knows a good thing when he sees it. He was the first in the city to put Ridgeview sparkling wine from the South Downs on his drinks menu and features Saddlescombe Farm lamb from just outside the city when in season, maybe served as a Slow-roasted shoulder with carrot-anise purée, kale, artichokes, roast potatoes and carrots.

Although long established, The Ginger Pig continues to change. "It has to evolve. Tastes have changed," says McKellar. "London coming down to Brighton has had a huge effect on the restaurant scene. Put duck hearts on back in the day and you wouldn't sell very many, now people lap them up. It's great."

The Ginger Pig

Crispy pig's head, kimchi, gochujang mayo

(Serves 4)

You will need to start this recipe the previous day, and the kimchi is best made a few days ahead, if you have time. Ask your butcher to clean the pig's head for you. You will have plenty of meat left over, but it freezes very well once portioned.

For the pig's head

½ pig's head, cleaned
2 carrots
1 onion
1 celery stick
½ garlic bulb
1 parsley sprig
½ bunch tarragon, chopped
200g flour
200ml milk
2 eggs
200g panko breadcrumbs
3 litres vegetable oil (or enough to fill a deep-fat fryer or ¾ fill a large pan)

For the kimchi

¼ head Chinese leaf, roughly shredded
2 garlic cloves, crushed
5g chilli flakes
10g anchovy fillets
20g carrots, julienned
1 tsp gochujang
10ml soy sauce

For the gochujang mayonnaise

150g mayonnaise
1 tsp gochujang
juice ½ lemon

Place the pig's head in a large pan with the carrots, onion, celery, garlic and parsley and cover with water. Bring to the boil, skim any impurities that rise to the surface, then simmer over a low heat for 6 hrs or until the meat falls easily off the bone. Remove the head, discarding the liquid and vegetables and allow to cool. Pick all the meat off the bone, keeping some of the fat and skin but not all of it. Add the chopped tarragon, season with salt and pepper, then tightly roll in cling film into a large sausage shape, twisting the ends to secure. Refrigerate overnight.

The next day, cut the sausage into 2cm slices. Set out 3 containers, one with the flour, one with the milk and eggs whisked together and one with the breadcrumbs. A few at a time, pass the slices first through the flour, then the milk and egg mix and finally the breadcrumbs, making sure they are well coated during each process. Refrigerate until ready to serve.

To make the kimchi, soak the Chinese leaf overnight in lightly salted water. Put into a clean tea towel and squeeze out as much water as possible. Combine with the remaining kimchi ingredients and adjust the seasoning. The flavour will improve if made a few days in advance.

To serve, make the mayonnaise by combining the ingredients in a small bowl. Heat the oil in a deep-fat fryer to 170°C and deep-fry the breadcrumbed pig's head pieces until brown, crisp and cooked through. Serve with the kimchi and mayonnaise.

Grilled asparagus with goat's cheese mousse

(Serves 4)

This is a lovely, light spring starter. Pheasant eggs are a good seasonal alternative to duck eggs and are available from April to June. You will need a gas-charged cream whipper for this dish.

For the goat's cheese mousse

150g goat's cheese
150ml milk
60ml olive oil
185ml double cream

To serve

skin from 4 chicken breasts, scraped clean of any fat
1 tsp white wine vinegar
4 duck eggs
12 asparagus spears, trimmed

To make the mousse, blend the goat's cheese with the milk and olive oil. Push through a fine mesh sieve into a bowl and stir in the cream. Pour into a cream whipper and charge with one gas bulb.

Heat oven to 180°C and line a baking tray with baking parchment. Lay the chicken skin flat in one layer, sprinkle with salt, then place another baking tray on top. Bake for 20 mins, then drain off any fat and return to the oven for a further 15 mins or until golden brown and crisp. Drain on kitchen paper and allow to cool, then break into large shards.

Bring a large pan of water to the boil and add the vinegar, then reduce to a gentle simmer. Crack the eggs into ramekins, then gently tip them into the simmering water, working quickly so they all cook at the same time. Poach for 3-4 mins until the whites are set but the yolks are still runny. Remove with a slotted spoon and drain on kitchen paper.

Grill the asparagus in a griddle pan over a high heat until charred all over.

To serve, arrange 3 asparagus spears, a duck egg and some of the chicken skin shards onto 4 plates, dispense some of the mousse from the whipper onto each plate and serve immediately.

Squid, nduja and potato salad

(Serves 4)

A quick and easy dish for a light supper or a dinner party starter. Nduja is a spreadable spicy salami from Calabria and is available from some supermarkets.

Cut open the squid tubes and lightly score the flesh in a criss-cross pattern. Slice into 6 pieces each.

Marinate the onion rings in the lemon juice, sugar and a pinch of salt for 1½ hrs.

Heat oven to 200°C. Cook the potatoes in boiling salted water for 15 mins or until soft. Drain, cut in quarters, place on a baking tray with the nduja and bake for 5 mins until the nduja begins to release its oils. Put in a bowl with the chicory and dress with the olive oil and some of the lemon juice to taste

Meanwhile, heat the vegetable oil in a pan to just below smoking point, season the squid with salt and pepper and fry for 1½ mins, finishing with a little lemon juice.

To serve, divide the potato, nduja and chicory between 4 plates and top with the squid.

2 medium squid tubes, cleaned
1 red onion, finely sliced into rings
50ml lemon juice
15g caster sugar
300g Jersey Royals or any salad potatoes
100g nduja
1 small head of chicory, finely sliced
50ml olive oil
juice 1 lemon
1 tbsp vegetable oil
½ bunch flat-leaf parsley

The classic combo of pork and apple taken to the next level by The Ginger Pig, recipe overleaf

2 x 300g pork fillets, trimmed of fat

For the pig cheek croquette

2 tbsp vegetable oil
6 pig cheeks
1 small onion, roughly chopped
1 carrot, roughly chopped
1 celery stick, roughly chopped
3 garlic cloves
125ml white wine
1 thyme sprig
500ml veal stock
500ml chicken stock
small handful chopped parsley
200g flour
200ml milk
2 eggs, beaten
200g panko breadcrumbs
3 litres vegetable oil (or enough to fill a deep-fat fryer or ¾ fill a large pan)

For the pickled apple

1 apple
100ml water
50ml white wine vinegar
20g caster sugar
1 bay leaf
1 thyme sprig

For the duck fat potato terrine

10 medium potatoes
250ml melted duck fat
handful chopped thyme

For the Jerusalem artichoke purée

600g Jerusalem artichokes, peeled and thinly sliced on a mandolin
150g unsalted butter
100ml double cream

To serve

5 tbsp butter
5 tsp vegetable oil
250ml cider
250ml pork or chicken stock
1 bunch cavolo nero, roughly chopped
100g Jerusalem artichokes, thinly sliced on a mandolin

Butter roast pork fillet, pig cheek croquette, duck fat potato terrine, cavolo nero

(Serves 4)

The duck fat potato terrine is a terrific accompaniment to the pork. It needs to be made a day ahead and will make about 15 portions, but will freeze well.

Slice each pork fillet into 2 equal pieces and tightly roll in cling film. Refrigerate until needed.

Make the croquette. Heat oven to 150°C. Heat the oil in a pan and seal the pig cheeks until brown all over. Remove to a plate, then brown the onion, carrot, celery and garlic in the same pan. Deglaze the pan with the white wine, then tip the contents of the pan into a large casserole dish with the thyme sprig, veal and chicken stocks. Cook in the oven for 2½-3 hrs or until the cheeks are very tender.

Remove the cheeks, then strain the cooking liquor through a fine sieve into a clean pan, discarding the vegetables and thyme. Reduce the liquor to make a thick, shiny sauce. Put the pig cheeks into a stand mixer with the sauce and parsley and very slowly mix with the paddle attachment until combined. Check for seasoning. Leave to cool in the fridge, then roll into 40g balls.

Set out 3 containers, one with the flour, one with the milk and eggs whisked together and one with the breadcrumbs. A few at a time, pass the croquettes first through the flour, then the milk and egg mix and finally the breadcrumbs, making sure they are well coated during each process. Return to the fridge.

To pickle the apples, scoop out balls of apple using a small Parisienne scoop. Put into a pan with the water, vinegar, sugar, bay, thyme and a pinch of salt and bring to the boil until the sugar has dissolved. Leave to cool. Transfer the pan contents to a vacuum-pack bag and seal in a vacuum-pack machine. Alternatively, simply pickle the apple in the liquor in a bowl.

To make the duck fat terrine, heat oven to 180°C. Line a cast-iron terrine mould with a double layer of cling film, leaving enough overhanging to cover the top. Thinly slice the potatoes on a mandolin. Layer up the potatoes in the terrine, adding a spoonful of duck fat, sprinkling of thyme and a pinch of salt to each layer. Cover with the overhanging cling film, place in a deep roasting tin, pouring in enough water to come halfway up the sides of the terrine mould, and bake for 1½ hrs or until a knife goes through the potatoes with no resistance. Allow to cool slightly, then place a heavy weight (ideally another terrine mould) on top and refrigerate overnight. Remove the cling film and cut into 1½-2cm slices.

To make the Jerusalem artichoke purée, put the sliced artichoke in a heavy-bottomed pan with the butter and a splash of water. Gently cook until soft, ensuring the artichoke doesn't colour. Add the cream and continue cooking to reduce slightly. Blend, adding a little more cream if the purée is too thick. Season with salt and pepper.

Heat oven to 180°C. Slice the pork into 4 portions, season with salt and pepper and pan-roast in 4 tbsp butter and 1 tsp oil until browned all over. Transfer to the oven and cook for 8 mins. Remove the meat and allow it to rest for a few mins (leave the oven on). Pour off the fat from the pan and deglaze with cider, then add the stock and reduce to a sauce consistency. Strain into a clean pan and keep warm.

Put 4 slices of potato terrine in a hot pan with the remaining oil and fry until golden brown on one side. Turn over the slices and place in the oven for 4 mins to finish warming through.

Heat the oil in a deep-fat fryer to 170°C. Meanwhile, fry the cavolo nero with the remaining butter and a little salt. Deep-fry the croquettes for 0 mins until golden brown and crisp. Remove and drain on kitchen paper while you deep-fry the sliced artichokes in the same oil until golden brown and crisp.

To serve, place a slice of terrine on 4 plates. Top with a half fillet of pork, sliced. Divide the cavolo nero between the plates and top with a croquette. Spoon some of the purée onto the plate and arrange the artichoke crisp and pickled apple around. Spoon over the sauce and serve.

Muscovado custard

(Serves 8)

550ml double cream
1 vanilla pod
8 egg yolks
150g muscovado sugar
15ml Oloroso sherry

For the crème fraiche sorbet

250g caster sugar
250ml water
500ml crème fraîche
zest 1 lemon

For the almond tuile

100g icing sugar
100g ground almonds
100g egg white
100g butter

Heat oven to 110°C. Bring the cream and vanilla to the boil in a pan, then remove from the heat. Beat the yolks together in a large bowl. Caramelise the sugar with 1 tbsp water in a pan until smoking, then carefully pour in the cream (the sugar will spit). Stir into the beaten eggs, then pour back into the pan and gently cook until the mixture starts to thicken. Once it has cooled slightly, stir in the sherry and pour the custard into 8 heatproof glasses (about 90ml per glass) and place in a deep roasting tin. Pour in enough water to come halfway up the sides of the glasses, then cook in the oven for 45 mins-1¼ hrs or until just set. Allow to cool completely, ideally overnight.

Make the sorbet by dissolving the sugar in the water in a pan to make a simple syrup. Allow to cool completely, then stir in the crème fraîche and lemon zest. Churn in an ice-cream machine and freeze until set.
To make the tuile, combine all the ingredients and allow to set in the fridge. Heat oven to 160°C. Thinly and evenly spread the tuile mixture onto a silicon mat or a baking tray lined with baking parchment and bake in the oven for 8 mins or until golden brown. Allow to cool, then break up into medium-sized pieces.

To serve, put a scoop of the sorbet into each glass on top of the custard and decorate with a tuile shard. At the restaurant, this dessert is also served with seasonal marinated fruit and fruit purée.

The Ginger Pig is renowned for its list of sherries, a passion of bar manager and bon viveur Rob Maynard and this elegant and simple dessert shows off the wonderfully fragrant, rich and nutty tones of Oloroso.

A margherita pizza emerges from the wood-fired oven at Fatto a Mano

Who doesn't love a pizza? It's one of the most popular - and most Instagrammed - foods in the world. According to the Oxford Companion to Food, the word 'pizza' was first used in Gaeta, a port between Naples and Rome, in 997AD. But modern pizza has its roots in Naples and dates back a century or so - and it's pizza Napoletana that's the inspiration behind Fatto a Mano, Brighton's home-grown group of authentic neighbourhood pizzerias.

Opened in London Road in August 2015 by Brighton-based chef Rupert Davidson (pictured far right), Fatto a Mano's wood-fired soft and pillowy pizzas were such an instant hit that a second, larger branch set over two floors and with an alfresco terrace opened in Hove a year later.

"Naples was always the inspiration for doing pizza the right way. They take the simplicity and produce so seriously, something I first saw when out there for a friend's wedding," says Davidson, who has worked in kitchens in the UK and internationally, including the Oxo Tower. He went on to become Development Director for restaurant and café operator Benugo before launching Fatto a Mano. "I couldn't get away from thinking that the UK pizza market had lost touch with the product, so we set out to create informal neighbourhood pizzerias centred around the wood-fired oven."

Although Fatto a Mano's roots are firmly in Italy, the classic cooking techniques of Naples and the produce of Campania, the restaurant looks closer to home for some of its ingredients. "We try to source products from Sussex wherever possible. Locally we work with some great suppliers including Barfield's butchers, Bison beer and Pharmacie Coffee," says Davidson.

He admits that perfecting Fatto a Mano's pizza dough recipe (see page209) took trial and error but the results have been worth it. Fatto a Mano's best seller is the classic Margherita, a personal favourite of Davidson's with its basil, mozzarella and tomato topping that mirrors the green, white and red of the Italian flag.

With a family-friendly menu that includes saltimbocca (filled pizza), calzone (folded pizza) and gluten-free options, Fatto a Mano's creed is as simple as its striking blue and white colour scheme. "Our name literally means 'made by hand' in Italian," explains Davidson. "Fatto a Mano is quite simply about great Neapolitan pizzas and developing an amazing team".

Fatto a Mano

Neapolitan pizza dough

(Makes 3 pizza bases)

This authentic Neapolitan-style pizza dough will take about 18-24 hrs to prove at an ambient temperature of between 18-23°C, so needs to be made a day ahead. Fresh yeast is available from any large supermarket bakery counter.

Dissolve the yeast in the water which should be lukewarm, about 22°C. Combine the flour and salt in a mixing bowl. Create a well in the flour, then pour in the water and yeast mixture in a few stages, combining with your fingertips to a moist dough (you may not need all the water).

Turn out the dough onto a floured work surface and knead for 8-12 mins until smooth and stretchy. Return to the bowl, cover with a damp cloth or cling film and leave to prove for around 12 hrs.

Turn out the dough onto a floured work surface and knead gently to knock it back slightly. Divide into 3 portions of about 210g each. Roll into balls, tucking the dough underneath so you have a smooth-topped ball. Place the three balls into a floured, deep-sided baking tray and cover with a damp cloth or cling film. Leave to prove for a further 6-12 hrs.

Heat oven to at least 220°C. Remove the proved dough by carefully slicing around each ball with a spatula, then sliding the spatula underneath each in turn and lifting away from the tray. Place onto a lightly floured surface and gently shape back into a round with your hands. Push out the dough into a 12in circle with your fingertips or use a rolling pin to achieve the same result. The dough should be 3-4mm thick.

Slide onto a metal baking sheet and add the toppings of your choice (see below). Bake for 4-6 mins or until the cheese has melted and the dough has coloured and cooked. Remove from the oven to a large plate and serve immediately.

0.2g fresh yeast
250ml water
380g plain flour, plus extra for dusting
10g salt

Pizza Margherita

There's nowhere to hide with this, the most classic and simple of pizzas. Use the best-quality ingredients you can find and you're in for a treat.

80ml San Marzano tomato sauce
(see page 213)
6 basil leaves
80g Fior di Latte or other good-quality
mozzarella
5g grated Parmesan
1 tsp extra virgin olive oil

Spread the tomato sauce evenly over the pizza base with the back of a spoon, then evenly place all the remaining ingredients across the base in the order listed. Season before cooking as above.

Pizza Norma
Vegetariana

This delicious pizza is lifted by a grating of incredible, deeply savoury Sardinian smoked ricotta just before serving.

80ml San Marzano tomato sauce
(see page 213)
50g diced and fried aubergine
35g fresh ricotta
6 basil leaves
80g Fior di Latte or other good-quality
mozzarella
5g grated Parmesan
1 tsp extra virgin olive oil
25g smoked ricotta

Spread the tomato sauce evenly over the pizza base with the back of a spoon, then evenly place all the remaining ingredients (except the smoked ricotta) across the base in the order listed. Season before cooking as above. Grate over the smoked ricotta before serving.

Pizza Salsiccia e Friarielli

White pizzas (with no tomato base) are popular in Naples and this is one of Fatto a Mano's best sellers. You can buy the restaurant's fennel and garlic sausages from Barfield's Butchers in Brighton.

60g pork, fennel and garlic sausage, cooked then skinned and crumbled
60g friarielli (Neapolitan broccoli) or cooked, cooled purple-sprouting broccoli or spinach
15g finely diced red chilli
6 basil leaves
80g Fior di Latte or other good-quality mozzarella
5g grated Parmesan
1 tsp extra virgin olive oil

Sprinkle the pork sausage over the pizza base, then evenly place all the remaining ingredients across the base in the order listed. Season before cooking as above.

Melanzane Parmigiana

(Serves 1-2)

This is a good portion for an individual meal served with garlic bread, or for two to share with a pizza. Fior di Latte is a type of mozzarella made with cow's milk which we source from Campania, but you can substitute any good-quality fresh mozzarella.

100ml olive oil
1 aubergine, cut into 8 x 1cm slices
260ml San Marzano tomato sauce (see below)
9 basil leaves
10g Parmesan, grated
40g Fior di Latte mozzarella, chopped

Heat oven to 200°C. Heat some of the olive oil in a large pan and fry the aubergine over a medium heat until browned, adding more oil as necessary.

Put one-third of the tomato sauce in the bottom of a 15cm x 4cm baking dish. Arrange 4 slices of aubergine over the sauce and season. Top with 4 basil leaves and sprinkle over half the Parmesan. Top with another third of the sauce, then the remaining aubergine. Sprinkle over the remaining Parmesan and basil leaves, and spoon over the remaining tomato sauce. Top with the Fior di Latte and bake for 15-20 mins until the cheese is bubbling and golden. Serve immediately.

Tomato sauce for pizza

Tinned San Marzano plum tomatoes are ideal but you can substitute good quality tinned plum tomato. At Fatto a Mano, nothing is added to the tomato so that it compliments the other pizza ingredients rather than overpowering them.

1 tin San Marzano plum tomatoes

Pulse the tomatoes in a food processor for a short time so that they retain some of their texture, you don't want a completely smooth puree. If using another brand of plum tomato, strain the excess juice through a sieve before processing.

Fatto a Mano's pizza dough recipe makes fantastic garlic bread, just spread the dough liberally with garlic butter and bake

What could be a better combination than the freshest seafood and the finest craft beer? Well, not much, according to Nick Jerrim who purchased a former neighbourhood boozer in Hove in 2015 and transformed it into The Urchin, a stylish bar and restaurant with a menu of fabulous fish and shellfish and a list of more than 100 craft beers from around the world.

"Shellfish has kind of gotten into the fine dining arena, but here we want it to feel like a dockside in a fishing village where you cook your mussels and eat them with your fingers with a couple of beers," says Australian-born Jerrim, a former DJ who moved to the UK in 1999 to manage nightclubs around the country, including Po Na Na in Brighton.

"We gave our chefs a remit that was very heavily influenced by my Australian roots: pan-Asian flavours which go really well with shellfish, plus this idea of finger food and fun. Our original chef, Sam Hutchins, had run a fish section in a restaurant in Sydney so got the idea immediately and just ran with it."

Hutchins left The Urchin in 2017, handing over the baton to former sous chef Rudy Jermaine Levi Perry (pictured right) who has continued to serve the pub's classic dishes such as Malaysian prawns and Shellfish bouillabaisse as well as putting his own spin on the regularly-changing list of specials. "Rudy's been with us since we opened, he's passionate about his different flavours so I can leave him to it," says Jerrim, who highlights Thai-style crab and Moules marinière as some of the pub's best sellers.

One of Jerrim's inspirations for The Urchin is Little Creatures brewery in Western Australia, where he worked for a year. "It's one of the leading craft brew places in the country. It's a big old brewery down on the marina and was a great experience. It broadened my tastes and gave me a real appreciation of things like Belgian, German and sour beers. And of course we've got Little Creatures beer on the shelf at The Urchin."

When it comes to the perfect seafood and craft beer combo, Jerrim doesn't hesitate. "When you finish a shift on a Friday and it's been a long day, it's nice to have Salt and pepper squid and some scallops with a strong IPA. That's always a winner for me."

The Urchin

GREEK STYLE MED
MUSSELS £11.50
WHOLE THAI CURRY CRAB
£16.50
WHOLE LOBSTER

Malaysian-style king prawns
(Serves 4)

This is a perennially popular dish at The Urchin and has been on the menu almost as long as the pub has been open. The blend of sweet and spicy ingredients adds lots of flavour without overwhelming the prawns, and makes a great addition to any Asian-style feast. You can peel the prawns before cooking, if you prefer, but it's much more fun to leave them on and get messy.

3 tbsp rapeseed oil
1 small onion, diced
4 garlic cloves, crushed
1½ tbsp mild curry powder
4 tbsp oyster sauce
3 tbsp sweet chilli sauce
500ml white wine or fish stock
30 shell-on king or tiger prawns
2 tbsp chopped coriander
4 spring onions, sliced
1 lime, cut into 4 wedges

Heat the oil in a large pan over a medium heat and sweat the onion and garlic for 2 mins. Add the curry powder and cook for a further 2 mins. Add the oyster sauce, chilli sauce and wine or stock, stir and bring to a simmer. Add the prawns and cook in the sauce until pink and firm. Divide between 4 serving bowls, sprinkle over the coriander and spring onion and garnish with a lime wedge.

Prawn and ginger wonton cups, ponzu dipping sauce

(Makes 12)

These spicy cups are another favourite at The Urchin and achieve maximum impact for minimum stress. They work equally well as a starter, canapé or part of a hot buffet.

Place the prawns and sesame oil in a food processor and pulse until coarsely chopped (you can also complete this step by hand with a sharp knife, just add the oil to the prawns after they've been chopped). Transfer to a bowl, add the ginger, chilli, coriander, fish sauce and black pepper, cover and refrigerate for 30 mins.

Lay a wonton wrapper onto a clean work surface. Place 1 tsp of the prawn mixture in the centre, wet the edges of the wrapper with a little water and draw the pastry up around the prawn mix. Using your thumbs and index fingers, seal the pastry around the prawn mix, shaping into a cup. Repeat until all the prawn mixture is used up. Set aside on a tray lined with greaseproof paper.

To make the dipping sauce, combine the rice vinegar, mirin, lemon juice, lime juice and soy in a bowl and stir well. The sauce will keep in the fridge, covered, for up to a week.

Cook the wontons in a bamboo steamer or in a shallow pan with a little water and a lid for 5 mins or until the prawn mix is pink and firm to the touch. Serve with the dipping sauce. At The Urchin, the cups are served on spiralised mooli (white radish) dressed with the dipping sauce and garnished with a little keta salmon caviar and micro-herbs such as baby coriander and baby basil.

12 king or tiger prawns, shelled and de-veined
1 tsp sesame oil
2 tbsp finely chopped pickled ginger
1 red chilli, deseeded and finely diced
2 tsp chopped coriander
3 tsp fish sauce
½ tsp black pepper
1 pack wonton wrappers (about 7cm square)

For the ponzu dipping sauce

50ml rice vinegar
180ml mirin
90ml lemon juice
90ml lime juice
160ml light soy sauce

Pan-seared scallops, truffle mash, balsamic shallots, crispy sage

(Serves 4)

Scallops are one of the biggest sellers at The Urchin. Here, they're treated as a luxury ingredient and paired with simple, honest flavours that don't detract from the shellfish's delicate sweet flavour. You may need to order king scallops in advance (ask for them in the shell to guarantee freshness and quality) but the extra effort and expense will be well worth it for a special occasion.

For the truffle mash

4 Maris Piper potatoes, diced
2 tbsp truffle oil
2 tbsp butter
1 tsp chopped parsley

For the balsamic shallots

1 tbsp rapeseed oil
4 banana shallots, sliced into ½cm rounds
2 tbsp caster sugar
150ml balsamic vinegar

For the crispy sage

250ml vegetable oil
12-15 sage leaves

For the scallops

12 king scallops, roe on, waste sack removed
1 tbsp butter
juice ½ lemon
baby coriander and basil leaves, to serve

First, make the mash. Cover the potatoes with cold water, add a pinch of salt and bring to the boil. Simmer until tender, then drain well. Add the truffle oil, butter and parsley, season with salt and pepper, then mash until smooth.

To make the balsamic shallots, heat the oil in a frying pan and arrange the shallots in a single layer in the pan. Fry for 4-5 mins until brown, taking care the shallots don't burn. Turn the shallots over so the cooked side is facing up, season with salt and pepper, sprinkle over the sugar and pour over the vinegar. Turn down the heat, cover the pan and simmer for 6-8 mins. Keep warm.

Make the crispy sage. Heat the oil in a pan and fry the leaves until the oil stops bubbling around the leaves – this means all their moisture has gone. Remove with a slotted spoon, drain on kitchen paper and season with salt.

Pat the scallops dry with kitchen paper and season on both sides. Heat a little oil in a large frying pan and place the scallops in the pan one at a time, going clockwise round the pan. Sear for 2 mins, then turn the scallops over in the order they went in the pan, first to last. Add the butter and lemon juice and cook for a further minute.

To serve, arrange 3 spoonfuls of mash on each plate and top each with a scallop. Place a crispy sage leaf into each spoonful of mash, then spoon some of the balsamic shallots with their cooking liquor around the plate. Finish with a sprinkling of herbs.

Twice-baked crab soufflé, spiced pear, Stilton mousse

(Serves 6)

This dish is all about pairing classic flavours, but with the volume turned up. Twice-baking eliminates the dreaded sunken soufflé syndrome, instead you're guaranteed a beautifully light but decadent dish that will impress at any dinner party.

For the soufflé

3 tbsp butter
200g breadcrumbs
2 tbsp rapeseed oil
1 red pepper, diced
3 spring onions, sliced
1 tsp smoked paprika
250g picked white crab meat
100ml white wine
1½ tbsp plain flour
125ml full-fat milk
3 eggs, separated
1 tbsp chopped parsley
4 tbsp double cream

For the spiced pears

2 pears, quartered, core removed
zest ½ orange
2cm piece root ginger, peeled and sliced
½ cinnamon stick
1 star anise
½ tsp ground allspice
½ tsp cloves
200ml white wine vinegar
175g caster sugar

For the mousse

150g Stilton
100g cream cheese
100ml double cream
1 tbsp chopped parsley

Heat oven to 180°C. Use 2 tbsp of the butter to grease 6 ramekin moulds, then line with the breadcrumbs. Heat the oil in a pan and sweat the peppers and spring onions for 2 mins until soft. Add the paprika and crab meat and stir well to combine. Pour in the wine and reduce completely. Leave to cool.

Melt the remaining butter in a pan over a medium heat, add the flour and cook for 2-3 mins, stirring continuously. Slowly pour in the milk and continue to stir until you have a thick, smooth béchamel sauce. Remove from the heat, stir in the yolks and parsley, and season with salt and pepper.

Whisk the egg whites to a stiff peak. Combine the crab mixture with the béchamel then, using a metal spoon, gently fold in the whisked whites. Divide the mixture between the ramekins, filling them to the top. Place in a deep roasting tin, pouring water into the tin so it comes halfway up the sides of the ramekins. Cook in the oven for 35 mins, then turn out the soufflés onto a wire rack to cool.

Put the pear quarters in a pan and cover with cold water. Bring to the boil and simmer until tender. Drain, reserving 300ml of the cooking liquid. Put the orange zest, ginger, cinnamon, star anise, allspice, cloves, white wine vinegar and caster sugar into a clean pan, add the reserved cooking liquid and bring to the boil. Pour over the cooked pears and allow to cool, then slice each quarter in half lengthways.

To make the mousse, blend the Stilton and cream cheese together until smooth. Whip the double cream to soft peaks, then fold into the Stilton mixture. Add the parsley, season with salt and pepper and transfer to a piping bag with a plain nozzle.

Put the soufflés on a baking tray and pour over the double cream. Return to the oven for 5 mins or until puffed up and golden. To serve, place a soufflé in the middle of a plate, arrange 2 slices of pear either side of the soufflé and pipe on dots of the mousse. Dress the plate with salad leaves and micro herbs such as baby basil or mustard frills.

Shellfish bouillabaisse with rouille

(serves 4)

The classic version of this traditional Provençal fish stew that originated in the French port city of Marseille normally calls for Pernod or pastis and uses quite robust fish, but for this shellfish version star anise delivers a sweeter aniseed flavour that complements the delicate shellfish. This is a great one-pot dish and would please any family as an alternative Sunday lunch. Other shellfish such as clams also work well.

For the fish stock

2-3kg fish bones, no heads
1 tbsp rapeseed oil
1 leek
1 white onion
1 fennel bulb
1 garlic bulb
4 bay leaves
10 star anise

For the bouillabaisse

3 tbsp rapeseed oil
1 onion, diced
1 leek, diced
1 fennel bulb, diced
2 bay leaves
pinch of saffron
5 star anise
3 tbsp tomato purée
50g green beans, cooked
10 new potatoes, cooked and sliced
1kg mussels, cleaned and de-bearded
4 langoustines
12 king prawns, peeled and de-veined
2 squid tubes, sliced into rings

For the rouille

½ baguette, crust removed and diced
100ml water
4 garlic cloves
1½ tsp smoked paprika
1 tsp chopped parsley
300ml olive oil

To serve

sliced and lightly toasted baguette

Make the fish stock by sweating the bones in the oil in a stock pot until translucent. Add the leek, onion, fennel, garlic, bay leaves and star anise and sweat for a further 5 mins or until the vegetables have softened. Cover with water and bring to the boil. Skim any impurities that rise, then turn down the heat and simmer gently for 25 mins. Strain through a large, fine-mesh sieve.

For the bouillabaisse, heat the oil in a deep pan, add the onion, leek, fennel, bay leaves, saffron and star anise and sweat for 8-10 mins, stirring occasionally. Add the tomato purée and cook for 4-5 mins then add the fish stock. Bring to the boil, then reduce the heat and simmer for 1½ hrs, stirring occasionally. Remove the bay leaves and star anise and, using a stick blender, blend the vegetables into the soup until smooth and thickened slightly. Season with salt and pepper.

To make the rouille, soak the bread with the water and allow to sit for 3-4 mins. Put all the ingredients in a food processor and blitz until a smooth, spreadable paste is achieved, then season with salt and pepper.

To serve, bring the soup back up to heat and add the green beans, potatoes, mussels and langoustines. Cover and cook for 2-3 mins until the mussels start to open. Add the prawns and squid and cook for a further 2-3 mins until the prawns are pink and firm. Serve in bowls with the baguette and rouille.

If you want the finest steaks in the city, head to this chic, buzzy restaurant that's tucked away down a side street between the Lanes and Brighton's central shopping area. You'll want to check out the specials board that features generous cuts of locally sourced meat such as Sussex Wagyu from Trenchmore Farm, all cooked to perfection in the restaurant's charcoal-burning Josper oven which reaches temperatures of 500°C.

But The Coal Shed is so much more than 'just' a great steak restaurant. Opened in 2011 by restaurateur Raz Helalat (formerly of The Ginger Pig, Helalat is also the owner of The Salt Room), The Coal Shed is also known for its menu of inventive modern British dishes. The kitchen was originally overseen by Dave Mothersill (who is currently head chef at The Salt Room and will soon open a second Coal Shed with Helalat in London), and been under the guidance of Henfield-born Matt Price (pictured right) since January 2016.

Although Price's CV is studded with Michelin stars, including Lords of The Manor, Gidleigh Park and Le Manoir aux Quat'Saisons, his path to the professional kitchen wasn't inspired by celebrity chefs. "I got into cooking to impress a girl. I started seeing someone who was really into food and her favourite thing was macarons. I spent a year mastering them at home and really got into cooking."

Price singles out a starter of Roast wood pigeon with boudin noir, bacon, parsnip and shimeji as indicative of his style, which fuses classical training with modern techniques. "This dish incorporates everything I really like - ingredients like great wood pigeon and amazing boudin noir. We use vacuum-pack techniques to pickle the mushrooms and we sous-vide the pigeon so that it's perfectly cooked, but the sauce is really old school."

With Sussex seafood, tomatoes from Nutbourne and foraged ingredients including sea herbs and wild garlic, Price keeps things local and seasonal but also incorporates influences from his travels in south-east Asia in dishes such as Asian braised saddleback pork with kimchi.

The Coal Shed

With a list of inventive cocktails such as a BBQ Sazerac made with rib-eye rye, demerara, absinthe and bitters, an eclectic and great-value wine list and one of the smartest private dining rooms in town, it's no wonder that The Coal Shed continues to be one of Brighton's most popular and successful dining destinations.

The Coal Shed

229

The perfect steak by Matt Price

We cook a lot of steak at The Coal Shed, however, the flavour imparted from our Josper grill is not something that can be recreated at home. You can cook a steak to perfection with ease if you follow these simple steps.

Select your meat carefully

Choosing your meat is every bit as important as cooking it right. It's worth spending a little extra on good quality, and buying meat less often rather than cutting costs. Quality points to look for:

Marbling

There should be a clean, white (or off-white) pattern of fat running through the meat. Don't confuse this with sinew or gristle. It will melt into the meat as it cooks, imparting moisture and, most importantly, flavour.

Fat

If selecting a cut with external fat, such as rump or sirloin, the fat or 'rind' should be crisp and dry. This indicates a dry-ageing process, imparting a deeper flavour to the meat.

Texture

The meat should be firm to the touch and slightly sticky, but never wet or flabby.

Colour

Look for a deep, dark red colour.

Warming the meat

Remove your meat from the fridge around half an hour before you cook it. This brings the core to room temperature, allowing a more even cook. Fridge-cold meat is easily undercooked or burned on the outside as you try to raise the internal temperature to the desired level.

Cooking

1. Season the meat well with sea salt and freshly cracked black pepper.
2. Sear in a very hot pan. Use a non-scented oil such as sunflower or rapeseed. It has a very high scorching temperature and will allow you to really caramelise the outside of the meat without burning.
3. When blood droplets appear on the top of the steak, turn over.
4. Add garlic and fresh thyme and cook for 1 minute

5. Remove most of the thyme and set aside.
6. Add a generous amount of butter.
7. Baste the streak with the garlic and thyme -scented butter.
8. Discard garlic and serve garnished with the reserved thyme. The meat will continue to cook after you remove it from the pan, so allow for a little more 'doneness' when you decide to remove from the heat.

Resting

This is crucial. Resting the meat allows the protein to relax and retain its moisture when carved. If the meat is not rested properly you will end up with a pool of blood and meat juice on your plate. Rest the meat for nearly as long you cook it for - it's well worth the wait.

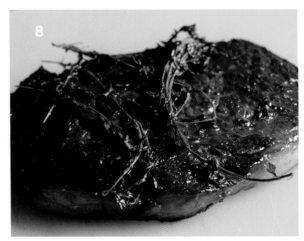

Béarnaise sauce

(Makes approximately 400ml)

This is a classic for a good reason. If done right, Béarnaise is the perfect steak accompaniment. Rich but acidic, it's worth doing the infusion in advance for great depth of flavour. Don't be put off by the method - it's straightforward and, with a little practise, it's a winner.

For the infusion

100ml white wine
100ml white wine vinegar
10g chervil sprigs
20g tarragon sprigs
50g finely sliced shallots
1 garlic clove, lightly crushed
10 black peppercorns

For the finished sauce

250g butter
3 egg yolks
½ tsp salt
juice 1 lemon
10g finely chopped tarragon

Place all infusion ingredients into a pan and put on a medium heat. Gently reduce by half. Pour into a sterilised Kilner jar. When sealed and refrigerated, this will keep for up to 1 month.

To finish the sauce, warm the butter over a low heat to clarify, skimming any solids that rise to the surface. Bring another saucepan of water to a simmer. Put the egg yolks, 50g of the vinegar infusion, strained through a fine sieve, and a pinch of salt into a mixing bowl and place over the pan of gently simmering water. It is important that the bowl does not contact the water. Whisk the egg yolks continuously so that they incorporate air, thicken and cook through. You are looking for thick ribbons of yolk that just hold their own weight.

Remove the bowl from the heat and gradually whisk in the warm clarified butter, leaving any sediment behind. It's important that the butter is warm as it will emulsify with the eggs better if they are the same temperature. Adjust the seasoning and acidity with salt and some of the lemon juice to taste, then stir in the chopped tarragon.

Pour the sauce into a container, and, if not using immediately, lightly press some cling film onto the surface to prevent a skin forming. Use the sauce within 1 hr and do not refrigerate.

Green peppercorn sauce

(Serves 2)

This is a 'pan sauce' i.e. made in the same pan you cooked your steaks in while they rest; it captures all the flavour of the meaty residue which also adds body and colour to the sauce.

25g butter
2 tsp green peppercorns
1 tbsp Cognac
1 garlic clove, finely diced
2 tbsp Dijon mustard
150ml whipping cream
½ lemon

Pour out most of the fat from the pan you have fried your steaks in but retain any clear juices. Add the butter, when it froths, add the peppercorns. Add the Cognac and ignite to burn off the alcohol (this step is optional) and then add the garlic and stir. Whisk in the mustard and cream and allow to simmer until the sauce will coat the back of a spoon. Adjust the seasoning (there will be salt and pepper in the pan already from cooking the steak) and add a squeeze of lemon juice to brighten the flavour.

The signature pigeon stater at The Coal Shed,
recipe overleaf

For the chicken jus

1kg chicken wings, chopped
1 onion, sliced
5 garlic cloves
100ml white wine
1 litre chicken stock
5 white peppercorns
20g tarragon
50ml double cream
10g thyme

For the parsnip purée

1kg parsnips
125g butter
200ml milk

For the herb oil

equal parts chervil, parsley and tarragon
vegetable oil

For the bacon crumb

4 rashers smoked streaky bacon

For the pickled shimeji

50ml white wine vinegar
50ml water
50g caster sugar
150g shimeji mushrooms, root removed,
mushroom trimmed

For the mushroom powder

dried porcini mushrooms

For the parsnip crisps

1 parsnip
3 litres vegetable oil (or enough to fill a deep-fat
fryer or ¾ fill a large pan)

For the pigeon

2 oven-ready wood pigeons
1 tsp vegetable oil
1 small bunch thyme
2 garlic cloves, lightly crushed
4 slices boudin noir, skin removed
25g butter

Roast wood pigeon, boudin noir, bacon, parsnip, shimeji

(Serves 4)

This dish has a bit of everything – acidity, sweetness, saltiness and an umami hit from the porcini powder. If you can source real French boudin noir it is well worth the effort – it's a highly spiced, super-smooth black pudding, and marries beautifully with the pigeon.

To make the jus, heat a little oil in a large saucepan, add the chicken wings and cook over a medium heat, stirring occasionally until they start to colour. Add the onions and garlic and continue to cook until the vegetables are totally soft and the wings are deeply caramelised. Add the white wine and scrape the bottom of the pan with a wooden spoon to deglaze. Simmer the wine until reduced by half, then pour in the chicken stock, peppercorns and tarragon. Bring back to a gentle simmer and cook for 45 mins, skimming the fat and sediment off the surface from time to time.

Double-strain the sauce first through a colander, then a fine mesh sieve into a clean pan. Add the double cream and thyme, then reduce quickly to your desired consistency to either a light jus or, if you prefer, a sticky, rich sauce. Strain again and keep warm.

To make the parsnip purée, peel the parsnips and cut into small dice. Heat a frying pan, and add the butter. Add the parsnips and cook over a medium heat, stirring occasionally, until tender and golden brown. Blend, adding as much of the milk as required to thin the consistency. Push through a fine mesh sieve and keep warm.

To make the herb oil, pick the herbs from the stalks and put into a pan. Cover with vegetable oil and bring to 80°C (use a heat probe to check the temperature). Blend and pass through a damp muslin cloth into a container. Refrigerate immediately to hold the oil's colour.

To make the bacon crumb, grill the bacon until very crisp. Allow to cool, then blitz to a fine crumb in a food processor.

To pickle the mushrooms, put the vinegar, water and sugar into a pan and warm until the sugar has dissolved, being careful not to boil. Allow to cool slightly, then pour into a container over the trimmed mushrooms.

To make the mushroom powder, heat oven to 100°C. Dry the mushrooms on a baking tray lined with baking parchment for 30 mins. Cool, then transfer to a pestle and mortar and grind to a fine powder.

Make the parsnip crisps. Heat the oil in a deep-fat fryer to 140°C. Peel the parsnip and discard the skin. Using the peeler, make long strips of parsnip and deep-fry until crisp. Season as soon as you remove from the fryer and blot any excess oil with kitchen paper.

Heat oven to 180°C. Make sure there are no scraps of feather attached to the pigeons. Season the birds all over with salt and black pepper. Heat the oil in a non-stick pan, add the birds, breast-side down, and cook for 1 min on each breast, caramelising evenly. Turn the birds cavity-side down in the pan, add the thyme and garlic and put in the oven for 5 mins. Remove the pan from the oven, add the boudin noir and butter and spoon the foaming butter over the crowns. Take the birds out of the pan and rest breast-side down for 5 mins. Finish cooking the boudin noir in the pan on the hob, then leave to rest with the pigeon for around 5 mins.

To serve, put a spoonful of warm parsnip purée onto 4 plates, off-centre. Take the pigeon breasts off the bone, season lightly and halve diagonally. Arrange the mushrooms, bacon, boudin noir and parsnip crisps in a semi-circle around the purée. Place the pigeon breasts on the purée, skin-side up. Sprinkle the mushroom powder onto the pigeon breast. Drizzle a little herb oil around the plate, then spoon over the chicken jus.

Charred octopus, ancho potato, padron peppers, squid ink aioli

(Serves 4)

This is one of the most popular starters at The Coal Shed. If you braise the octopus carefully it becomes very tender; don't be daunted by it, it's fairly simple to cook and finish. Squid ink is available from fishmongers including Brighton and Newhaven Fish Sales on Hove Lagoon.

1 fennel bulb, finely sliced
1 onion, finely sliced
1 garlic bulb, halved
2 tbsp vegetable oil
25g fennel seeds
10g cumin seeds
10g coriander seeds
10g black peppercorns
5 star anise
50g sweet smoked paprika
5g ground ancho chilli
250ml red wine
10g chicken bouillon powder
1.5kg octopus

For the ancho potato croquette

2 baking potatoes
1 shallot, very finely diced
1 garlic clove, finely crushed
10g dried ancho chilli, finely chopped
25g butter
zest 1 lemon (reserve the juice for the aioli)
1 egg yolk plus 2 whole eggs
1 pack panko breadcrumbs
3 litres vegetable oil (or enough to fill a deep-fat fryer or ¾ fill a large pan)

For the chorizo butter

150g good-quality cooking chorizo, skin removed, meat coarsely chopped
25g sweet smoked paprika
250g butter, diced

Squid ink aioli

100g mayonnaise
1 tsp squid ink
5g garlic, finely chopped and minced
juice 1 lemon

To serve

12 Padron peppers, halved

Heat oven to 140°C. In a non-stick pan, roast the fennel, onion and garlic in 1 tbsp oil until golden. In a separate frying pan, dry-fry the fennel, cumin, coriander, peppercorns and star anise until they release their aroma. Tip them into a piece of muslin cloth and tie into a bag with kitchen string. Put the onion and fennel mix into a casserole along with the spice bag, paprika, chilli, wine, bouillon and octopus. Cover with water and stir. Put the lid on the casserole and cook in the oven for 2½ hrs, or until the tentacles are very tender. Allow to cool in the stock.

Increase the oven to 180°C. Cover a small roasting tray with table salt, prick the potatoes with a fork and place the potatoes on the salt. Bake for 1¼ hrs or until cooked through.

While the potatoes are baking, sweat the shallots, garlic and ancho chilli in the butter over a low heat, stirring often until the shallot is very soft. Add the lemon zest.

While the potatoes are still warm, scoop the flesh from the skins (wear rubber washing-up gloves to protect your hands from the heat) and push through a mouli or potato ricer. Add the shallot mix and egg yolk, then adjust the seasoning. Transfer to a piping bag and pipe in lines onto a tray lined with greaseproof paper. Set in the freezer, then cut into croquettes. Whisk the whole eggs together with a fork, then one by one roll the croquettes in the egg, then the breadcrumbs and then the egg and breadcrumbs once more.

Make the chorizo butter by blitzing the chorizo and paprika in a food processor, scraping down the sides of the bowl periodically. When smooth, add the butter, a piece at a time, until well incorporated.

Make the aioli by combining all the ingredients in a bowl. Adjust the acidity with some of the reserved lemon juice to taste.

Using a pair of kitchen scissors, remove the octopus tentacles as close to the head as possible.

Heat a non-stick pan and cook the tentacles in the remaining vegetable oil, turning as they start to crisp. Add a good knob of chorizo butter and continue to cook until the butter is caramelised. Remove the octopus and allow to rest. Deglaze the pan with a few spoonfuls of the octopus cooking stock.

Heat the oil in a deep-fat fryer to 180°C and deep-fry the croquettes until crisp. Drain on kitchen paper. Grill the Padron peppers until the skin starts to blister.

Place a spoonful of aioli on 4 serving plates, then arrange the peppers around. Place a croquette off-centre on each plate, and lay an octopus tentacles across it. Spoon some of the chorizo butter sauce over the octopus and around the plate to serve.

1 hogget loin

For the boulangère potatoes

6 baking potatoes, finely sliced using a mandolin
50g chopped thyme
1 litre homemade lamb stock, or 2 lamb stock cubes dissolved in 1 litre boiling water
50g butter

For the faggot

250g minced lamb
50g lamb's liver, very finely chopped
10g finely chopped thyme
5g garlic, finely crushed
1 egg yolk
250ml red wine
1 tsp red wine vinegar
1 pack panko breadcrumbs
1 tbsp vegetable oil
250ml lamb stock

For the pearl barley

100g pearl barley
1 tsp vegetable oil
1 banana shallot, peeled but root attached
2 garlic cloves
100ml white wine
10g thyme sprigs
500ml lamb stock, or 1 lamb stock cube dissolved in 500ml water

For the baby carrots

8 baby carrots, stalks trimmed
1 orange
10g sugar
1 tarragon sprig

To serve

1 head of broccoli, cut into florets

Loin and faggot of hogget, boulangère, pearl barley, baby carrots

(Serves 4)

Hogget is a sheep aged between 1-2 years old with the characteristic tenderness of lamb but more flavour. You should be able to find it in most good butchers; ask them to take the loin from the saddle for you.

To make the boulangère, heat oven to 165°C. Line a roasting tray with greaseproof paper. Layer the potatoes in the tray, overlapping slightly, from left to right. Season lightly with salt, pepper and some of the thyme. Turn the roasting tray 90 degrees, then lay the next layer of potatoes left to right. Continue this pattern until all the potato has been used. Pour over the lamb stock, and dot the butter on top.

Cover with baking parchment and bake for 1 hr or until the potatoes are very tender. Remove from the oven, place a second roasting tray on top of the boulangère and weigh it down with something heavy (tinned food works well). Leave to press and cool for 1 hr, then refrigerate overnight with the weights still in place.

To make the faggots, put the mince, liver, thyme, garlic and egg yolk in a bowl. Reduce the wine in a pan over a medium heat to 50ml, then add to the faggot mix. Combine everything well by hand without
overworking the mix. Add the vinegar and enough of the breadcrumbs so that the mix comes together without being too dry. Roll into golf ball-sized pieces and chill until ready to cook.

Prepare the pearl barley by washing under running water in a sieve. Heat the oil in a non-stick saucepan over a medium heat and cook the shallot and garlic until caramelised. Add the white wine and thyme and reduce by 80%, scraping the pan to deglaze. Add the pearl barley and stock, season lightly and simmer very gently until just tender. Remove the pan from the heat and allow to cool in the stock so the barley absorbs the flavour from the cooking liquid. Cool.

To cook the carrots, peel the orange with a potato peeler and juice it. Put the orange skin, juice, carrots, sugar and tarragon into a pan and add just enough water to cover. Place over a low heat and simmer very gently until the carrots are just tender.

To serve, gently pan-fry the faggots in the oil until caramelised. Add the lamb stock and continue to cook, spooning the sauce over the faggots until they are glazed and sticky.

Heat oven to 180°C. Remove the boulangère from the roasting tray and cut into rectangles. Heat a non-stick pan and caramelise 4 portions of the boulangère on the top and bottom, then transfer to the oven until warmed through.

Cut the hogget loin into 4 portions, scoring the fat well. Cook fat-side down in a pan over a medium heat, rendering the fat until crisp. Turn the loin over, cook for a couple of minutes on the flesh, then remove from the pan and rest.

Blanch the broccoli in a pot of boiling salted water, then drain and arrange around 4 plates. Warm the pearl barley through, removing the shallot, garlic and thyme. Place a small pile on each plate, and place the hogget loin on top. Place the boulangère and glazed faggots around the plate. Heat the carrots in their cooking liquid, drain and arrange on the plate. Spoon a little of the glaze from the faggots around the plate and serve.

The humble banana elevated to the gastronomic heights, recipe overleaf

2 bananas
1 tsp lime juice
150ml double cream
80g egg whites
100g caster sugar

For the candied pecans

250g pecan halves
250g sugar
250ml water
3 litres vegetable oil (or enough to fill a deep-fat
fryer or ¾ fill a large pan)

For the maple tuile

100ml isomalt
75ml glucose syrup
25ml maple syrup

For the dulce de leche mousse

240ml double cream
125g dulce de leche
80g pasteurised egg white
10g icing sugar

Malt cake purée

200g butter
250g golden caster sugar
100g Greek yoghurt
3 eggs
seeds from 1 vanilla pod
125g Ovaltine
200g self-raising flour

To serve

4 slices pain d'epices
2 bananas
caster sugar

Banana iced parfait, pecan, maple, dulce de leche

(Serves 6)

This parfait makes a lovely homemade ice cream substitute without the hassle of having to churn it. You can buy pain d'epices – a type of French cake - in most good French delicatessens.

Heat oven to 180°C. Roast the bananas in their skins until the skin starts to split and liquid starts escaping. Scoop out the flesh and blend with the lime juice. Push through a fine sieve into a mixing bowl.

In a separate bowl, lightly whip the double cream. Blend the egg whites and sugar in a stand mixer to make a semi-stiff meringue. Fold the banana purée into the double cream, then whisk in 1/3 of the meringue. When incorporated, carefully fold in the remaining meringue, retaining as much volume as possible. Either pipe into moulds or spoon into a plastic tub. Freeze for 6 hrs.

For the pecans, heat the oil in a deep-fat fryer to 180°C. Heat the sugar and water in a pan over a high heat until the sugar dissolves. Drop in the nuts and cook until the sugar reaches 118°C (check the temperature with a heat probe or sugar thermometer). Drain immediately, then deep-fry for 1 min. Allow to cool then roughly chop, reserving 12 halves to decorate the parfaits.

To make the tuile, heat oven to 180°C. Put the isomalt, glucose syrup and maple syrup into a very clean, dry pan. Cook to 160°C (check the temperature with a heat probe or sugar thermometer). Immediately pour onto a silicon pastry mat and allow to cool. When totally cold, transfer to a blender and whizz to dust. Using a sieve, dust some of the maple pow-der back onto a silicon mat and bake for just 20-30 secs. Allow to cool, then lift from the mat. Break into shards and store between sheets of baking parchment in a sealed container.

Make the mousse by lightly whipping the double cream and folding in the dulce de leche. Whisk together the egg white and icing sugar, then mix with the cream mixture. Pour into a cream whipper and charge with 2 gas bulbs.

Heat oven to 170°C. Make the malt cake purée by creaming the butter and sugar together until light and fluffy. Mix in the yoghurt, then the eggs one by one followed by the vanilla. Dissolve 50g Ovaltine in 2 tbsp boiling water and add to the mixture. Sift the flour with a pinch of salt and fold in. Line a baking tin with baking parchment, pour in the cake mixture and bake for 45 mins or until a knife pushed into the middle of the cake comes out clean.

Allow to cool slightly, remove from the tin and break up the cake into a blender. Put the remaining Ovaltine in a heat-proof jug and pour over 200ml boiling water. Stir well, then gradually add to the blender as it's running to achieve a glossy and shiny purée the consistency of thick caramel. Cool, then transfer to a piping bag.

To serve, grill the pain d'epices until very dry and crisp. Allow to cool, then grind in a pestle and mortar. Halve the bananas lengthways, then cut into segments. Sprinkle the flat side liberally with the caster sugar and, using a blowtorch, brûlée the sugar until golden brown.

Remove the parfaits from the freezer 10 mins before serving (if using moulds, otherwise scoop individual portions straight from the freezer). Place 1 parfait off-centre on 6 serving plates and decorate with 2 pecan halves. Arrange the chopped pecans, pain d'epices crumb and malt cake purée around the parfait. Arrange a few banana segments on each plate, then siphon some dulce de leche mousse around the plate. Finish with shards of maple tuile.

"Every coastal town deserves a Riddle and Finns," said respected food writer Tom Parker Bowles in his Daily Mail review of the restaurant. Well, lucky old Brighton has got two: the original in the Lanes with its white tiled walls, sharing tables with high stools, chandeliers and busy open kitchen, and a second in a converted arch on the beach complete with open-air terrace and sea views. Both serve oysters, crustacea, heaving platters of fruits de mer and a selection of starters, salads and mains that feature the finest sustainable local and British seafood.

"I went to the Swan Bay Oyster Company, an old-school Italian-run mom-and-pop kind of place in San Francisco where you sit at the counter side-by-side and eat shellfish. There were people queuing out the door and I just thought, this is a winner," says Rob Shenton (pictured right) who opened Riddle and Finns in 2007 in what was the Lanes Pasta Shop with business partner Adam Brian and chef Patrick Timpson.

"I worked for Patrick when I was 17 in my hometown of Stoke-on-Trent. He brings a lot of experience to the professional kitchen, trains the younger chefs in fish preparation and works with me on the menus." Shenton's first venture in Brighton was Due South, which came to national press attention when it opened in 2004 for its local and seasonal approach. "We continued to run both Due South and Riddle and Finns for a period of time, but felt Due South's USP had been diluted with other places doing local food so we decided to focus on one brand rather than two."

With Due South transformed into Riddle and Finns on the beach, both restaurants serve an inclusive menu designed to appeal to all tastes. "The idea is to create an accessible and relaxed but slightly up-scale restaurant that people can either come to and eat mackerel and chowder, or drink Champagne and eat oysters. We have really established things like lobster thermidor and fish pie to more modern things like sashimi and Singapore chilli crab, which is something I cooked a lot when I worked in Australia for a year."

And that slightly puzzling name? "Riddle is a technique in Champagne production and Finns refers to the fish. We felt the true spelling with one n was a bit weird and aesthetically it looks better with two."

Riddle and Finns

Fruits de mer

(Serves 6)

This opulent dish captures the quintessence of Riddle and Finns' character; a visually gorgeous, bulging feast on a platter, overflowing with a medley of the best, most colourful and mouthwatering seafood that requires little embellishment. This is a simplified version that's easier to cook at home – at the restaurant the platter includes prawns, winkles, whelks, razor clams and crayfish.

2 x 600g lobsters
1kg brown crab
10 langoustines (optional)
300g mussels
300g clams
10 oysters, freshly shucked

For the mayonnaise

2 medium egg yolks
5g Dijon mustard
2 pinches each sea salt and ground white pepper
250ml grapeseed oil
1 tsp white wine vinegar
2 tsp lemon juice

For the shallot dressing

80g banana shallots, finely chopped
100ml red wine vinegar
chopped leaves 1 tarragon sprig

lemon wedges, to serve

Put the lobsters in the freezer for 2 hrs to render them unconscious. Place the crab in a large pan of boiling water, bring back to the boil and simmer for 10 mins. Remove the lobster from the freezer and push an oyster knife through the cross-like marking on the top of the lobster. Add to the pan with the crab and continue to simmer for a further 15 mins, adding the langoustines, if using, in the last 3 mins of cooking. Remove, place on a tray and allow to cool.

(recipe continues overleaf)

Riddle and Finns

Remove the claws and legs from the main body of the crab and crack them with a large chef's knife so the meat can be easily removed by your guests. Pull the main body of the crab from the shell and, using a spoon, scrape all the brown meat from the head into a bowl. Using a seafood pick, remove the white meat from the body into a separate bowl. Cover the picked crab meat and refrigerate until needed.

Prepare the cooked lobsters by removing the tail and cutting it in half lengthways, keeping it in the shell. Remove the intestines from the middle of the tail. Crack the claws with the blade of a large chef's knife and reserve in the fridge.

Wash the mussels and clams in cold running water, drain and remove any barnacles and beards. Get a bowl of iced water ready. Put into a large saucepan with 50ml water, cover with a lid and cook over a very high heat for 1 min or until the shellfish starts to open. Drain, then plunge into the iced water. Open the mussels and clams, keeping the flesh in the half shell. Reserve in the fridge.

Make the mayonnaise by whisking together the egg yolks, mustard and salt and pepper in a large mixing bowl. Add the the oil in a steady trickle, whisking energetically until the oil is absorbed and the mixture turns pale yellow and thickens, usually after adding about 150ml of the oil. Thin down the consistency with the vinegar and lemon juice, then whisk in the remaining oil. Taste and correct the seasoning if necessary, then refrigerate in a covered container until needed.

Make the shallot dressing by mixing the shallots, vinegar and tarragon together in a small bowl.

To serve, arrange the cooked shellfish and oysters on a platter and garnish with edible seaweed and lemon wedges. Serve with fresh mayonnaise and good crusty bread and the shallot dressing for the oysters.

Pan-seared scallops, butternut squash, parma ham crisp

(Serves 4)

12 king scallops, roe on
1 butternut squash
8 slices Parma ham
1 tbsp olive oil
100g peas, cooked
1 bag pea shoots
4 tsp white truffle oil

Heat oven to 200°C. Wash the scallops under cold running water and dry on kitchen paper. With a small knife, trim off the muscle (the band of white flesh that attaches the scallops to their shells). Refrigerate until needed.

Wrap the squash in tin foil and roast for 40 mins-1 hr or until soft. Whilst still hot, scoop out the flesh, avoiding the seeds, and blend until smooth. Put the blended squash in a fine sieve with a container underneath and leave to drain for 1 hr.

Put the Parma ham on a baking tray lined with baking parchment and place in the previously heated oven until the ham is dark and crisp, turning once during the cooking (timing will vary according to the ham and your oven so keep a close eye on the ham while it's cooking). Allow to cool.

Heat a small non-stick pan to smoking point, then turn down to a medium heat. Season the scallops with fresh cracked black pepper and sea salt. Fry in the oil for 1 min per side until caramelised.

Spread some of the butternut squash across 4 serving plates and arrange 3 scallops on each plate. Arrange 2 pieces of the ham, a few of the peas and the pea shoots around and season the dish with a few drops of the truffle oil.

We also serve scallops with lemon and parsley sauce. Cook the scallops as above, then add 100ml fish stock to deglaze the pan and a knob of butter. Swirl the pan to emulsify the sauce, add a squeeze of fresh lemon juice and some freshly chopped parsley and serve with a fresh rocket and fennel salad. Other variations include chorizo and chilli with coriander, bacon lardons and even Guinness in place of the fish stock.

Seafood, smoky ham and subtly sweet squash make for a dish that's very simple to prepare, pleasing to the eye and wonderful to eat.

Lobster salad

(Serves 4)

A beautiful salad that's perfect for the summer. Simple and light with fresh citrus fruits and mango, the colour contrast is amazing, and it's a great dish to impress friends. Buy ready-cooked lobsters if you prefer to not cook them yourself.

2 lobsters
1 lemon, halved
1 garlic bulb, halved
1 small bunch lemon thyme
1 small bunch rosemary
2 bay leaves
1 star anise
1 orange
1 pink grapefruit
1 mango
1 tbsp caster sugar
100ml olive oil
100ml olive pomace oil
generous selection salad leaves
8 king prawns, cooked and shelled

Put the lobsters in the freezer for 2 hrs to render them unconscious. When ready to cook the lobster, put the lemon, garlic, thyme, rosemary, bay and star anise in a large pan, cover with plenty of water and bring to the boil to make a court bouillon.

Remove the lobster from the freezer and push an oyster knife through the cross-like marking on the top of the lobster. Get a bowl of iced water ready. Cook the lobster in the court bouillon for 10-12 mins, depending on its size. Remove and plunge into an ice bath to stop the cooking and retain flavour.

Segment the orange and grapefruit, reserving the trimmings. Peel and slice the mango, reserving the stone. Put the trimmings and stone in a pan, cover with water and add the sugar. Bring to the boil and reduce by half to create a sticky, sweet and slightly bitter syrup. Strain through a sieve into a bowl and leave to cool. Whisk the oils into the syrup and season to taste to make the dressing.

Remove the lobster meat from the shells, retaining the shells for presentation. To serve, put the leaves, citrus fruits, mango, lobster meat and prawns in a mixing bowl, spoon over enough of the dressing to coat and divide between 4 plates. Decorate with the lobster shells and serve.

Riddle and Finns famous fish pie

(Serves 8)

A great dish to be enjoyed all year round. With its creamy Pernod-infused sauce and grilled fish topped with buttery mash, it's food for the soul.

1 lemon thyme sprig
2 bay leaves
1 tsp vegetable oil
4 tbsp chopped banana shallots
120g butter
140g plain flour
80ml Noilly Prat
40ml Pernod
400ml milk
60ml double cream
500ml fish stock
1kg potatoes, diced
3 egg yolks
500g white fish fillet of your choice, lightly grilled
300g salmon fillet, lightly grilled
3 hard-boiled eggs, peeled and quartered
200g leeks, white parts only, blanched and roughly chopped
100g peas, blanched
125g Parmesan
125g fresh breadcrumbs
1 small bunch parsley, leaves picked and chopped
1 lemon, zest only

Tie the thyme and bay leaves with kitchen string into a bouquet garni, then fry in the oil with the shallots over a medium heat until the shallots are soft. Add the butter and cook until it starts to bubble but not burn. Turn down the heat and add the flour. Whisk until a smooth paste forms (the base of a roux sauce), then flambé the Noilly Prat and Pernod into the paste mix. Keep stirring until the flames die down, then slowly whisk in the milk and cream.

(recipe continues overleaf)

Riddle and Finns

Slowly pour in the fish stock and cook for a further 20-30 mins on a low heat to cook out the flour. Season with salt and pepper to taste (if you'd like more of a kick to the sauce, now is a good time to add a little Dijon mustard or chilli to taste). While the sauce is cooking, put the potatoes in a large pan, cover with water and bring to the boil. Add salt and simmer for 15 mins or until tender. Drain, mash, season with salt and pepper and stir in the egg yolks.

Heat oven to 180°C. Strain the sauce through a fine mesh sieve into a large rectangular pie dish and break in the grilled white fish and salmon. Evenly add the egg, leeks and peas and top with the potatoes (using a piping bag with a star nozzle to get a delicate edging which will brown nicely in the oven). Grate over the Parmesan and scatter over the breadcrumbs. Bake in the oven for 30 mins or until browned and bubbling. To serve, top with the parsley and lemon zest.

At the restaurant, the pie is cooked and served in individual ramekins baked for 15 mins and topped with prawns and served with mangetout, green beans and kale and a fennel and rocket salad.

Chocolate marquise

(Serves 8)

A smooth and light dark chocolate mousse on a chocolate crumb base, glazed with silky dark chocolate and cream, this is a perfect dessert to show off your pastry skills.

500g digestive biscuits
3 tsp cocoa powder
260g butter
250g dark chocolate callets (chips)
5 eggs, separated
100g caster sugar

For the chocolate glaze

2 gold gelatine leaves
100ml water
170g caster sugar
75g cocoa powder
90ml double cream

To make the base of the marquise, blend the biscuits and cocoa
powder together to a fine breadcrumb consistency. Melt 80g of the butter, add to the crumb and mix well to a paste. Press this paste 0.5cm deep into 8 individual cylinder moulds set on a baking
parchment-lined baking sheet and refrigerate to set.

Melt the chocolate chips with the remaining butter in a bain marie over a low heat, stirring occasionally until all the chocolate has melted. Remove from the heat. Whisk the egg yolks and 50g of the sugar over a bain marie on a low heat - removing occasionally from the heat during this process to avoid scrambling the eggs - until the mixture coats the back of a spoon and forms ribbons. Remove from the heat.

Whisk the egg whites and remaining sugar together to stiff peaks. Fold the melted chocolate into the yolk mixture, then fold in the egg whites. Pour into a piping bag and rest for 5-10 mins in the fridge. Pipe into the prepared moulds stopping 1-2mm from the top, then refrigerate for 1 hr.

To make the glaze, soak the gelatine in water until soft. Put the remaining glaze ingredients in a solid bottom pan and slowly bring to the heat, but don't boil as this can burn the cocoa and make a bitter glaze. Squeeze out as much water as you can from the gelatine, add to the glaze mix on the stove and stir until the gelatine has melted. Pour into a container to cool slightly (it needs to be warm enough to pour but not so hot that it will melt the dessert).

Remove the set marquise from the fridge and set over a cooling rack. Heat the moulds gently with a blowtorch so that they will easily slide off. Spoon the glaze over the desserts 1 tbsp at a time, using the back of the spoon to evenly coat the marquise on the top and sides. Return to the fridge for 30 mins-1 hr or until the glaze is set. At the restaurant, the marquise is served with rich chocolate ice cream, pistachio crumb and macaroons.

Fourth and Church

Is it a wine bar? A wine shop? A restaurant? In fact, the distinctly individual Fourth and Church is all three, and its owners are similarly multi-disciplined. Sam Pryor (pictured far right) has worked as a bar manager and assistant manager of a hotel (and took a four-year break from hospitality to work in the off-shore renewables industry) while Paul Morgan (pictured right) has managed restaurants and hotels. Both have extensive experience as chefs. The pair originally met in 1996 at Terre à Terre in Brighton where Pryor was washing pots and Morgan was head chef. Their paths crossed again over a decade later at Pelham House Hotel in Lewes, where they began to hatch plans to open their own place.

"Although we enjoy more formal restaurants, the meals that we most remember are evocative of a place and a culture where there's lots of sharing, and we bonded over the love of that style of food," says Pryor, who opened Fourth and Church with Morgan (with a little help from well-known local wine merchant and bon viveur Henry Butler) in October 2015.

Perusing the list of small plates on the short, ever-changing menu while you sit among shelves lined with exciting wines and a counter serving house-cured salt beef sandwiches to the lunchtime trade, you wouldn't guess that Pryor spent two years cooking at The Fat Duck and similarly cutting-edge WD50 in New York.

"We use some techniques like low-temperature cooking, and I did a lot of experiments on brining at The Fat Duck, but the greatest influence from that time was how you use processes to create the flavours that you want while respecting the ingredients," says Pryor, who takes the lead on the food side of the operation, leaving Morgan to concentrate on the wines. "We create our own artisan products, be they spice mixes, ferments, pickles or charcuterie. They're the building blocks of our recipes."

Drawing on the 'cucina povera' of France, Spain and Italy, the menu might feature boldly flavoured dishes like Warm brandade of smoked haddock with black olives and fennel or a simple plate of Salted and marinated Cantabrian anchovies. "Fourth and Church is a place where you can enjoy good wines and good food in a relaxed environment," says Pryor. "It's somewhere that showcases great products that are treated sympathetically and with a bit of intelligence, without being intimidating."

Fourth and Church

Pumpkin Tirshi, yogurt, coriander, black sesame za'atar

(Serves 4)

This is a great dip or meze dish that's delicious eaten with warm flatbreads. You can use any type of squash or pumpkin, although cooking times may vary. You will have harissa paste left over which can be stored covered with a slick of oil for up to two weeks, or more in the fridge. It's very versatile and excellent with roast meat, fish and vegetables. Similarly, leftover za'atar will keep for a month in an airtight container.

For the harissa

200g large red chillies, sliced
50g salt
1 litre water
2 garlic bulbs, peeled
250ml olive oil
1 tbsp urfa chilli flakes
1 tbsp ground cumin
1 tbsp ground caraway

For the za'atar

50g black sesame seeds
50g sesame seeds
1 tsp sumac
2 tsp dried oregano
1 tsp chopped fresh thyme
2 tsp ground fennel seed

For the Tirshi

500g pumpkin, cut into 1-inch cubes
200ml water
40ml olive oil
1 tbsp chopped preserved lemon
1 tsp ground cumin
1 tsp ground coriander
1 tsp paprika
juice 1 lemon

To garnish

150ml yogurt
1 bunch coriander

To make the harissa, first ferment the chillies. Make a brine by heating the salt and water together in a pan until the salt dissolves, then leave to cool. Place the brine and the sliced chillies in a plastic container and cover loosely with a damp cloth. Leave at room temperature for 48 hrs or until the liquid has a pleasing sourness (it may need a further 24-48 hrs depending on the temperature of the room and the lactic bacteria on the chillies). Refrigerate, ensuring the chillies remain submerged in the brine.

Place the garlic cloves in a pan in one layer and cover with oil. Heat slowly until the oil gently bubbles, then reduce the heat as low as possible and cook - stirring to ensure the garlic doesn't stick - until just soft but not falling apart. Leave to cool in the pan, then transfer the garlic and the oil to a container and refrigerate. Combine the drained chillies and garlic with 100ml of the oil, chilli flakes, cumin and caraway in a blender and blitz until smooth.

To make the za'atar, toast the sesame seeds in a dry pan and add the sumac, oregano, thyme and fennel seed.

Cook the pumpkin slowly in a pan with the water until the water has evaporated and the pumpkin is starting to fall apart. Add the oil and cook, breaking up the pumpkin with a wooden spoon until it forms a paste but with some texture left. Stir in 3 tsp harissa, the preserved lemon, cumin, coriander, paprika and lemon juice and season with salt and pepper.

To serve, spread the pumpkin Tirshi over 4 plates with a spoon. Sprinkle over the za'atar, dot with the yogurt and garnish with coriander leaves.

Oysters Rockefeller, fennel, Veronese speck

(Serves 4)

This is a fantastic, rich dish for a special occasion. It can be served at brunch, as the fish course at a dinner party or as a starter - just adjust the number of oysters per person.

24 oysters
65g spring onions, chopped
130g parsley
15g sorrel
100g watercress
2 tbsp pastis
125g butter
2 tsp Tabasco
10g tarragon
10g chervil
175g white bread, dried in a low oven

For the fennel salad

2 fennel bulbs
50ml olive oil
juice ½ lemon

To garnish

80g speck, thinly sliced and cut into ½ cm ribbons
leaves ½ bunch chervil

Carefully open the oysters with an oyster knife, straining the brine into a container.

Bring 5 litres of water to the boil with a pinch of salt and prepare a large bowl of iced water.
Blanch the spring onions for 1 min, then remove to the iced water. Repeat the process with first the parsley, then the sorrel and watercress, blanching each for 20 secs (the aim is to bring the herbs and vegetables to temperature as quickly as possible and then chill down quickly to preserve the green colour and stop cabbage-like flavours developing). Remove from the ice bath and squeeze dry in a clean cloth.

Make the Rockefeller butter by heating the pastis, butter, Tabasco and 50ml of the reserved oyster brine until the butter has just melted. Leave to cool until it reaches blood heat. Put the sorrel, watercress and 55g parsley along with the tarragon and chervil into a blender, add the butter mixture and blitz until smooth. Refrigerate until needed.

Clean the blender, then blitz the remaining parsley and bread to a fine green crumb.

Finely shave the fennel and toss with the olive oil and lemon juice, season with salt and pepper and drain on kitchen paper to remove excess dressing.

To finish the dish, remove the Rockefeller butter from the fridge half an hour before using to soften. Heat the grill. Pipe or spoon over the oysters and top with a thin layer of crumbs. Grill the oysters for 5 mins until the crumb starts to brown. To serve, mix the fennel salad with the speck and chervil and place a small pile on each oyster.

Beetroot gravadlax, dill crème fraîche, caperberries

(Serves 4)

You'll need to plan ahead several days to make the gravadlax but it's worth it for a rich, buttery and deeply-flavoured treat. This recipe makes more gravadlax than you need, but you get a better result curing a larger piece of fish - plus the leftovers are delicious with brown bread and butter or scrambled eggs and toast. Ask your fishmonger for a piece of salmon from the head end rather than the tail, cut from a large fish to ensure you have a nice thick even fillet.

For the salmon cure

250g coarse sea salt
250g granulated sugar
finely grated zest 1 lemon
1 tsp fennel seeds
1 tsp coriander seeds
250g beetroot, peeled and finely diced
600g thick salmon fillet, skin on

For the salmon topping

1 bunch dill, chopped
zest 1 lemon, finely grated

For the dill crème fraîche

1 bunch dill, chopped, reserving a little to serve
200g full-fat crème fraîche

1 lemon, cut into 4 wedges
12 caperberries

To make the cure, blitz all the ingredients apart from the salmon in a food processor, scraping down the sides of the bowl until you have a coarse paste. Lay out a double thickness of strong, good quality cling film large enough to completely wrap the fish and spread out half of the paste in the rough shape of the salmon fillet. Lay the fillet on top, skin-side down, and carefully spoon over the remainder of the cure. Parcel up the cling film, place in a plastic container and refrigerate for 36 hrs. Unwrap the cling film and empty the cure into the container. Place the salmon back into the cure, skin-side up, submerging the flesh. Leave for another 12 hrs.

Wash the cure off the salmon under running water (the flesh should be bright pink), then blot dry with kitchen paper. Lay the salmon on a double layer of cling film and top with an even covering of chopped dill and lemon zest. Parcel up the salmon and place in a clean plastic container. At this point the salmon should mature for at least 2 days and can be kept for 2 weeks if wrapped well and refrigerated.

To serve, mix the chopped dill into the crème fraîche. Slice the finished salmon gravadlax as thinly as possible with a very sharp knife. Allow at least 5 slices per person. Divide the slices between 4 serving plates, grind over some black pepper and top with a spoonful of the dill crème fraîche. Garnish each plate with lemon wedges, caperberries and dill.

For the chicken stock

2kg chicken bones
2 carrots, roughly diced
2 celery sticks, roughly diced
1 onion, roughly diced
2 thyme sprigs
2 parsley sprigs
4 litres water

For the braised lamb

1.5kg piece bone-in lamb shoulder
1 tbsp olive oil
2 fennel bulbs, roughly diced
1 onion, roughly diced
2 tbsp coriander seeds, toasted
2 tbsp fennel seeds, toasted

For the lamb sauce

2 tsp finely diced preserved lemon
2 tsp finely diced pickled red chillies

For the pickled quince

1 quince
juice ½ lemon
100ml white wine vinegar
100g sugar
2 cloves
1 cinnamon stick
1 star anise
6 peppercorns

For the mint oil

½ bunch mint, leaves only
½ bunch flat-leaf parsley, leaves only
150ml olive oil

For the confit potatoes

300g red-skinned potato, cut in 1cm dice
250ml vegetable oil (or enough to cover the potatoes)

To serve

1 tbsp olive oil

Crispy lamb shoulder, mint, pickled quince, pomegranate

(Serves 4)

This is a complex recipe but one that results in a crisp and deeply savoury lamb dish with fresh, aromatic herb and spice accents. This is a useful dish for a dinner party as all elements can be made a day ahead with the only tasks left being a quick sauté and heating through of the sauce before you serve.

Make the chicken stock a day ahead. Heat oven to 180°C. Put the bones into a large roasting tin – don't crowd the tin so use two if necessary as you are trying to achieve a nice even golden brown. Roast for 40 mins-1½ hrs depending on your oven. Place the roasted bones in a large stock pot and deglaze the roasting tin on the hob with 200ml water, scraping up the residue. Add to the pot with the vegetables, thyme and parsley, cover with 4 litres water and bring to the boil. Reduce the heat and simmer for 4 hrs, skimming the surface regularly with a ladle to remove any scum. Strain through a fine sieve into a clean pan and reduce the stock over a high heat to 2 litres.

Heat oven to 120°C. Sear the lamb shoulder in a hot pan with the olive oil until dark brown on all sides, then transfer to a casserole dish or pan that just fits the piece of meat. Cover with some of the stock and add the diced vegetables, coriander and fennel seeds. Cover tightly with tin foil and cook for 4 hrs or until fork-tender. Leave the pan to cool, then drain off the liquid into a container and refrigerate until chilled. Shred the lamb with two forks and set aside until ready to start the sauté.

To make the sauce, remove the chilled braising liquid from the fridge and discard the solidified fat. Over a high heat in a pan, reduce the sauce to 400ml, then transfer to a blender and blitz with the preserved lemon and chilli. Refrigerate until ready to use.

To make the pickled quince, peel the fruit, cut into 1cm dice and place in a container with water and lemon juice. Put the peelings and core in a pan with the white wine vinegar, sugar, cloves, cinnamon, star anise and peppercorns. Add 100ml cold water, bring to the boil then reduce the heat and simmer for 20 mins. Remove from the heat and allow to cool and infuse for 10 mins. Drain the quince and add to a clean pan, straining the pickling liquid over the quince. Bring to the boil, reduce the heat and simmer for 20 mins. The quince can be refrigerated in a container for up to a month.

For the mint oil, bring a large pan of water to a rolling boil and blanch the mint and parsley for 30 secs. Drain and refresh in iced water. Squeeze the herbs dry with kitchen paper, then blitz in a blender with the olive oil.

Place the potatoes in a pan in a single layer and cover with the oil. Heat slowly until the oil starts to bubble gently, then reduce the heat to the lowest it will go. Cook for 30 mins or until the potatoes are just soft but not falling apart, stirring to ensure that they don't stick. Leave to cool in the pan, then transfer with the oil to a container and refrigerate.

To finish the dish, heat a large frying pan until very hot, add the olive oil and confit potatoes. As soon as they begin to brown, add the lamb shreds and sauté over a medium-high heat until the lamb starts to crisp. Add the pomegranate seeds, spring onions, mint and coriander leaves and season with salt and pepper. Heat the sauce and whisk in 4 tbsp mint oil. Pile the sauté into the centre of 4 bowls and pour the sauce around.

The cheesecake that's inspired by a salad,

recipe overleaf

Innes goat's curd cheesecake, baked apple, honey, lemon thyme

This dish utilises the affinity of ingredients most often served together as a salad but which also work well as a dessert by using a mild curd such as Innes goat's curd from Highfields Dairy Farm in Staffordshire. Caramelising the walnuts is a tricky job, and care should be taken with hot sugar as it can cause nasty burns if it comes into contact with skin.

425g Innes goat's curd
200ml cream
3 egg yolks
25g sugar

For the pickled grapes

100ml Spanish brandy
25ml Pedro Ximinez sweet sherry
100ml red wine vinegar
125g sugar
½ bunch seedless red grapes, halved lengthways

For the caramelised walnuts

20 walnut halves
400g white sugar

For the baked apple purée

3 large Cox's apples
½ tsp malic acid
50g white sugar

To garnish

4 lemon thyme sprigs, leaves only
honey

Heat oven to 120°C. Whisk together the curd, cream, yolks and sugar with a pinch of salt until homogenous; try to not incorporate too much air. Butter a 5cm-deep, 12cm-square cake pan, line with baking paper and pour in the cheesecake batter. Cook until just set but with a slight wobble, around 40 mins. Refrigerate for at least 4 hrs.

Combine the brandy, sherry, vinegar and sugar with 250ml water in a pan and bring to the boil. Simmer for 20 mins then leave for 5 mins to cool slightly. Add the grapes and decant to a suitable container. The grapes will keep for a few weeks in the fridge.

Heat oven to 180°C. Roast the walnuts on a baking tray until golden. Heat the sugar in a non-stick pan, stirring continuously until the sugar has melted and caramelised to a golden brown. Stop the sugar cooking by placing the base of the pan in a basin of cold water. Return the pan to a low heat and dip the still-hot nuts, one by one, into the caramel with a fork. Place onto an oiled baking sheet, ensuring that each nut is covered with caramel. Monitor the heat to ensure that the caramel doesn't overheat and burn or cool and harden.

To make the baked apple purée, heat oven to 180°C. Core the apples and wrap in tin foil. Bake for 40 mins or until soft. Blitz in a blender with the malic acid and sugar, adding water if necessary to make a thick purée. Push the purée through a fine sieve with the back of a ladle and store in a container in the fridge.

To serve, cut the cheesecake into fingers. Place a good blob of the purée on each plate. Top with the cheesecake, place the pickled grapes and caramelised nuts around the plate, sprinkle with lemon thyme and dot with honey.

Restaurant directory

64 Degrees
53 Meeting House Lane, BN1 1HB
01273 77011; 64degrees.co.uk

Bincho Yakitori
63 Preston Street, BN1 2HE
01273 779021; binchoyakitori.com

The Chilli Pickle
17 Jubilee Street, BN1 1GE
01273 900383; thechillipickle.com

The Little Fish Market
10 Upper Market Street, Hove, BN3 1AS
01273 722213; thelittlefishmarket.co.uk

The Set
33 Regency Square, BN1 2GG
01273 855572; thesetrestaurant.com

Cin Cin
13-16 Vine Street BN1 4AG
01273 698813; cincin.co.uk

Plateau
1 Bartholomews, BN1 1HG
01273 733085; plateaubrighton.co.uk

The Salt Room
106 King's Road, BN1 2FU
01273 92948; saltroom-restaurant.co.uk

Silo
39 Upper Gardner Street, BN1 4AN
01273 674259; silobrighton.com

Semolina
15 Baker Street, BN1 4JN
01273 697259; semolinabrighton.co.uk

The Gingerman
21A Norfolk Square, BN1 2PD
01273 326688; gingermanrestaurant.com

Terre à Terre
71 East Street, BN1 1HQ
01273 729051; terreaterre.co.uk

Curry Leaf Café
60 Ship Street, BN1 1AE
01273 207070; curryleafcafe.com

Isaac At
2 Gloucester Street, BN1 4EW
07765 934740; isaac-at.com

The Ginger Pig
3 Hove Street, Hove BN3 2TR
01273 736123; thegingerpigpub.com

Fatto a Mano
77 London Road BN1 4JF
01273 600621; fattoamanopizza.com

65-67 Church Road, Hove BN3 2BD
01273 325400; fattoamanopizza.com

The Urchin
15-17 Belfast Street, Hove BN3 3YS
01273 241881; urchinpub.wordpress.com

The Coal Shed
8 Boyce's Street, BN1 1AN
01273 322998; coalshed-restaurant.co.uk

Riddle and Finns
12b Meeting House Lane, BN1 1HB
01273 721667; riddleandfinns.co.uk

139 King's Road, BN1 2FN
01273 821218; riddleandfinns.co.uk

Fourth and Church
84 Church Road, Hove, BN3 2EB
01273 724709; fourthandchurch.co.uk

Brighton's Best Restaurants

Founded in 2015, Brighton's Best Restaurants is run by three friends who live in the city, love its restaurant and food culture and want the world to know about it. In addition to the annual Brighton's Best: Top 20 Restaurants awards, Brighton' Best organise and promote OctoberBEST, an annual festival where the top 20 restaurants offer specially created £20 menus. Find out more at www.brightonsbestrestaurants.com

Patrick McGuigan is a Brighton-based freelance food journalist, who contributes regularly to titles including The Telegraph, The Financial Times, Harrods Magazine and Restaurant, among many others. One of the country's foremost cheese writers, Patrick hosts regular tastings for the public and judges at international cheese awards. He is one of the founders of the London Cheese Project - a two-day festival celebrating the British cheese renaissance.
@PatrickMcGuigan patrickmcguigan.com

Andy Lynes is a freelance food, drink and travel journalist and author. His work appears regularly in the national press. He was one of the first people in the world to blog about food and is a Masterchef semi-finalist. He teaches food writing at Leith's School of Food and Wine in London and is working on his first novel, set in the restaurant industry.
@andylynes andylynes.com

Euan MacDonald is a founder and restaurant reviewer for 60secondreviews, that reviews restaurants old and new in short videos. This has also led him to work for Hardens and the Guild of Fine Food on the annual Great Taste Awards. He's also the co-founder of Winebox.tv with Brighton wine legend Henry Butler. He lives a few doors up from the Gingerman, a block away from Bincho Yakatori, and close to The Set and at the time of publication is not barred from any of them.
@euanmac60 60secondreviews.com

Index

Page references for photographs are in **bold**

A

Aged beef fillet, foie gras, white asparagus 148, **149**
Apple: Caramelised apple, flapjack and cinnamon ice cream **188**, 189
Asparagus: Grilled asparagus with goat's cheese mousse 194, **195**
Aubergine:
Grilled aubergine with miso **26**, 27
Melanzane Parmigiana **212**, 213

B

Baked hara chutney mackerel 174, **175**
Barbecue red-spiced bream 42, **43**
Beef:
Aged beef fillet, foie gras, white asparagus 148, **149**
Beef cheek, Marmite mash, turnip **68**, 70
Beef rib, carrot, crumb 16, **17**
Braised ox cheek, patty pans, tarragon **122**, 123
Ox cheek, turnip, Paris browns 98, **99**
Sirloin steak, egg yolk and beetroot ketchup 186, **187**
The perfect steak 230
Banana iced parfait, pecan, maple, dulce de leche **242**, 244
Basil panna cotta, strawberry, pistachio, black pepper 102, **103**
Bass:
Line-caught bass, brandade stuffed piquillo pepper, Umbrian lentils **56**, 57
Béarnaise sauce 232
Beetroot:
Beetroot gravadlax, dill crème fraîche, caper-berries 268, **269**
Venison, beetroot, walnut 18, **19**
Better batter and lemony Yemeni relish 162
Blood orange, white chocolate, cookie **72**, 74
Blue cheese: Chimchimney soufflé and sooty tops **158**, 160
Bouillabaisse: Shellfish bouillabaisse with rouille 226, **227**
Bum (cheesecake) 166, **167**
Bream: Barbecue red-spiced bream 42, **43**
Broccoli:
Grilled tenderstem broccoli with sesame and apple 24, **25**
Veal, smoked broccoli, kohlrabi and purple kale **184**, 185
Butter roast pork fillet, pig cheek croquette, duck fat potato terrine, cavolo Nero **198**, 200
Butternut payasam 177

C

Caramelised apple, flapjack and cinnamon ice cream **188**, 189
Carrot tartare 66, **67**
Cauliflower:
Korean fried cauliflower 156
Roasted cauliflower and wild garlic 180, **181**

Cereal milk 76, **77**
Celeriac: Slow-baked celeriac with black truffle and Castelfranco 84, **85**
Charred octopus, ancho potato, padron peppers, squid ink aioli 238, **239**
Cheesecake:
Bum 166, **167**
Peanut butter cheesecake, dark chocolate sorbet **136**, 137
Innes goat's curd cheesecake, baked apple, honey, lemon thyme **272**, 274, **275**
Chicken:
Chicken stock 65
Chicken nuggets, red cabbage ketchup 64, **65**
Japanese fried chicken 30, **31**
Roasted poussin, carrot gnocchi, ginger broth 132, **133**
Southern fried chicken 170, **171**
Turbot, roast chicken, sherry, morels 58, **59**
Chimchimney soufflé and sooty tops **158**, 160
Chocolate:
Chocolate marquise 260, **261**
Chocolate truffles 115
Dark chocolate pavé, popcorn ice cream 150, **151**
Nougat glace, passionfruit, chocolate 60, **61**
Peanut butter cheesecake, dark chocolate sorbet **136**, 137
Pecan and white chocolate cannoli 152, **153**
Churrosimo 164, **165**
Clams:
Fruits de mer 248, **249**, 250, **251**
Surfboard 112, **113**
Cod:
Cod with truffle pomme purée and red wine sauce **146**, 147
Line-caught bass, brandade stuffed piquillo pepper, Umbrian lentils **56**, 57
Skrei cod, potato purée, brown shrimp, brown butter **54**, 55
Crab:
Crab, radish and wasabi salad 28, **29**
Crab scotch egg, curry mayonnaise, apple 106, **107**
Fruits de mer 248, **249**, 250, **251**
Twice-baked crab soufflé, spiced pear, Stilton mousse 224, **225**
Shellfish moily 40, **41**
Surfboard 112, **113**
Crispy lamb shoulder, mint, pickled quince, pomegranate 270, **271**
Crispy pig's head, kimchi, gochujang mayo 192, **193**
Cured and smoked Sussex coast mackerel, cucumber, wasabi 142, 143, **145**

D

Dark chocolate pavé, popcorn ice cream 150, **151**

Doughnuts:
Churrosimo 164, **165**
Doughnuts 114
Soya milk doughnuts, Hoji-cha ice cream 34, **35**

F

Fazzoletti with wild garlic pesto, sheep's milk ricotta and toasted almonds 90, **91**
Fish pie, Riddle and Finns famous 256, **257** 258, **259**
Fruits de mer 248, **249**, 250, **251**
Fudge:
Nutella fudge 114
Peanut butter fudge **136**, 137

G

Garlic bread 214
Goat's cheese:
Innes goat's curd cheesecake, baked apple, honey, lemon thyme **272**, 274, **275**
Green peppercorn sauce 232, **233**
Grilled asparagus with goat's cheese mousse 194, **195**
Gulab jaman: Pistachio kulfi and gulab jaman 48, **49**
Gurnard:
Gurnard, octopus and olives **110**, 111
Raw gurnard, oyster, broccoli 120, **121**

H

Halloumi: Better batter and lemony Yemeni relish 162
Ham hock pakoras, masoor dal, yoghurt 94, **95**
Hispi, hollandaise, truffle **14**, 15
Hogget: Loin and faggot of hogget, bou-langère, pearl barley, baby carrots 240, **241**

I

Innes goat's curd cheesecake, baked apple, honey, lemon thyme **272**, 274, **275**

J

Japanese fried chicken 30, **31**
K
Keralan mussel moilee **172**, 173
Korean fried cauliflower 156

L

Lamb:
Crispy lamb shoulder, mint, pickled quince, pomegranate 270, **271**
Lamb cannon, braised tongue, sweetbreads, wild garlic risotto 100, **101**
Loin and faggot of hogget, boulangère, pearl barley, baby carrots 240, **241**

Langoustine:
Fruits de mer 248, **249**, 250, **251**
Surfboard 112, **113**
Lentil, swede and Medita samosas, rhubarb chutney 134, **135**
Line-caught bass, brandade stuffed piquillo pepper, Umbrian lentils **56**, 57
Linguini with mussels and nduja 88, **89**
Lobster:
Fruits de mer 248, **249**, 250, **251**
Lobster salad 254, **255**
Loch Duart salmon, posh potato salad, fennel 52, **53**
Loin and faggot of hogget, boulangère, pearl barley, baby carrots 240, **241**

M
Mackerel:
Baked hara chutney mackerel 174, **175**
Cured and smoked Sussex coast mackerel, cucumber, wasabi 142, **143, 145**
Malaysian-style king prawns 218, **219**
Melanzane Parmigiana **212**, 213
Monkfish: Raw monkfish, pickled onions, tiger's milk 108, **109**
Muscovado custard 202, **203**
Mushrooms: King oyster mushrooms, rosemary, celeriac 118, **119**
Mussels:
Fruits de mer 248, **249**, 250, **251**
Keralan mussel moilee **172**, 173
Linguini with mussels and nduja 88, **89**
Shellfish moily 40, **41**
Surfboard 112, **113**

N
Neapolitan pizza dough **208**, 209
Nougat glace, passionfruit, chocolate 60, **61**

O
Octopus:
Charred octopus, ancho potato, padron peppers, squid ink aioli 238, **239**
Gurnard, octopus and olives **110**, 111
Ox cheek:
Braised ox cheek, patty pans, tarragon **122**, 123
Ox cheek, turnip, Paris browns 98, **99**
Oysters:
Oysters Rockefeller, fennel, Veronese speck 266, **267**
Fruits de mer 248, **249**, 250, **251**
Raw gurnard, oyster, broccoli 120, **121**
Surfboard 112, **113**

P
Pan-seared scallops:
with butternut squash, Parma ham crisp 252, **253**
with truffle mash, balsamic shallots, crispy sage 222, **223**
Panna cotta:
Basil panna cotta, strawberry, pistachio, black pepper 102, **103**
Cereal milk 76, **77**
Pasta:

Fazzoletti with wild garlic pesto, sheep's milk ricotta and toasted almonds 90, **91**
Linguini with mussels and nduja 88, **89**
Peas: Sweetcorn and green pea vadas 176
Peanut butter:
Peanut butter cheesecake, dark chocolate sorbet **136**, 137
Peanut butter ice cream 115
Pecan and white chocolate cannoli 152, **153**
Pig's head: Crispy pig's head, kimchi, gochujang mayo 192, **193**
Pigeon: Roast wood pigeon, boudin noir, bacon, parsnip, shimeji **234**, 236
Pistachio kulfi and gulab jaman 48, **49**
Pizza:
Neapolitan pizza dough **208**, 209
Pizza Margherita 210
Pizza Norma vegetarian 210
Pizza salsiccia e friarielli 211
Pollock, Jerusalem artichoke and nasturtium 182, **183**
Pork:
Crispy pig's head, kimchi, gochujang mayo 192, **193**
Butter roast pork fillet, pig cheek croquette, duck fat potato terrine, cavolo Nero **198**, 200
Pork knuckle vindaloo **44, 46**, 47
Pork momos **38**, 39
Slow-cooked belly pork **32**, 33
Poussin: Roasted poussin, carrot gnocchi, ginger broth 132, **133**
Prawns:
Malaysian-style king prawns 218, **219**
Prawn and ginger wonton cups, ponzu dipping sauce **220**, 221
Surfboard 112, **113**
Pumpkin Tirshi, yogurt, coriander, black sesame za'atar 264, **265**

R
Rabbit crochette with fresh pesto 80
Raw gurnard, oyster, broccoli 120, **121**
Raw monkfish, pickled onions, tiger's milk 108, **109**
Raw salmon, watermelon, cucumber, dashi 96
Rhubarb:
Rhubarb curd meringue tart, buttermilk ice cream 138
Rhubarb, lemon, shortbread **20**, 21
Yorkshire rhubarb, raw cacao, lemon thyme 126, **127**
Riddle and Finns famous fish pie 256, **257**, 258, **259**
Risotto: Lamb cannon, braised tongue, sweetbreads, wild garlic risotto 100, **101**
Roast wood pigeon, boudin noir, bacon, parsnip, shimeji **234**, 236
Roasted cauliflower and wild garlic 180, **181**
Roasted poussin, carrot gnocchi, ginger broth 132, **133**

S
Salmon:
Loch Duart salmon, posh potato salad, fennel 52, **53**

Raw salmon, watermelon, cucumber, dashi 96
Sardines: Salad of pickled sardines, blood orange and puntarella 86, **87**
San Marzano tomato sauce 213
Scallops:
Pan-seared scallops, butternut squash, Parma ham crisp 252, **253**
Pan-seared scallops, truffle mash, balsamic shallots, crispy sage 222, **223**
Shellfish moily 40, **41**
Surfboard 112, **113**
Sea bream, miso cauliflower, black sesame 130, **131**
Sea buckthorn, brown butter, Douglas fir 124, **125**
Sheep's milk cheese: Bum (cheesecake) 166, **167**
Shellfish:
Fruits de mer 248, **249**, 250, **251**
Shellfish bouillabaisse with rouille 226, **227**
Shellfish moily 40, **41**
Sirloin steak, egg yolk and beetroot ketchup 186, **187**
Skrei cod, potato purée, brown shrimp, brown butter **54**, 55
Slow-baked celeriac with black truffle and Castelfranco 84, **85**
Slow-cooked belly pork **32**, 33
Southern fried chicken 170, **171**
Soya milk doughnuts, Hoji-cha ice cream 34, **35**
Squid, nduja and potato salad **196**, 197
Steak:
The perfect steak 230, **233**
Sirloin steak, egg yolk and beetroot ketchup 186, **187**
Surf board 112, **113**
Sweetcorn and green pea vadas 176

T
Taste of the Pier 114
The perfect steak 230, **233**
Tomato: San Marzano tomato sauce 213
Tuna, passionfruit, radish 12, **13**
Turbot, roast chicken, sherry, morels 58, **59**
Twice-baked crab soufflé, spiced pear, Stilton mousse 224, **225**

V
Veal, smoked broccoli, kohlrabi and purple kale **184**, 185
Venison, beetroot, walnut 18, **19**
Vindaloo:
Pork knuckle vindaloo **44, 46**, 47

W
Wood pigeon:
Roast wood pigeon, boudin noir, bacon, parsnip, shimeji **234**, 236

Y
Yorkshire rhubarb, raw cacao, lemon thyme 126, **127**

Chef Publishing Ltd
FS Building
Dormer Road
Thame
Oxfordshire
OX9 3FS

© Chef Publishing Ltd
The rights of the author have been asserted. All rights
reserved. No part of this book may be reproduced, stored in a
retrieval system or transmitted in any form or by any means,
electronic, electrostatic, magnetic tape, mechanical,
photocopying, recording or otherwise, without the prior
permission in writing of the publisher.
ISBN 978-1-908202-99-4

Text © Andy Lynes 2017
Photography © Peter Marshall 2017 except:
Alun Sperring portrait page 37 © Julia Claxton
Thierry Pluquet and Vincent Lebon portrait page 93 and Silo
food images pages 118-127 © Xavier D. Buendia
/XDBPhotography
Isaac Bartlett-Copeland portrait page 179 © Gill Copeland
All recipes are © of the respective restaurants
The Urchin recipes pages 218- 227 written by Sam Hutchins

Andy Lynes has asserted his right under the Copyright,
Designs and Patents Act, 1988, to be identified as Author of
this work.

Brighton's Best logo © Brighton's Best Restaurants

Publisher Peter Marshall
peter@chefpublishing.com
Editor: Andy Lynes
Sub editor: Suzanne Lindfors
Photographer: Peter Marshall
Designer: Roman Gavriush
Printed by Novyi Druk
All the food featured in the book was prepared for
photography by the chefs at their restaurants